Old King Cole

A Pantomime

Paul Reakes

A Samuel French Acting Edition

SAMUELFRENCH-LONDON.CO.UK
SAMUELFRENCH.COM

Copyright © 2012 by Paul Reakes
All Rights Reserved

OLD KING COLE is fully protected under the copyright laws of the British Commonwealth, including Canada, the United States of America, and all other countries of the Copyright Union. All rights, including professional and amateur stage productions, recitation, lecturing, public reading, motion picture, radio broadcasting, television and the rights of translation into foreign languages are strictly reserved.

ISBN 978-0-573-16448-4

www.samuelfrench-london.co.uk

www.samuelfrench.com

FOR AMATEUR PRODUCTION ENQUIRIES

UNITED KINGDOM AND WORLD
EXCLUDING NORTH AMERICA
plays@SamuelFrench-London.co.uk
020 7255 4302/01

Each title is subject to availability from Samuel French,
depending upon country of performance.

CAUTION: Professional and amateur producers are hereby warned that OLD KING COLE is subject to a licensing fee. Publication of this play does not imply availability for performance. Both amateurs and professionals considering a production are strongly advised to apply to the appropriate agent before starting rehearsals, advertising, or booking a theatre. A licensing fee must be paid whether the title is presented for charity or gain and whether or not admission is charged.

The professional rights in this play are controlled by Samuel French Ltd, 52 Fitzroy Street, London, W1T 5JR.

No one shall make any changes in this title for the purpose of production. No part of this book may be reproduced, stored in a retrieval system, or transmitted in any form, by any means, now known or yet to be invented, including mechanical, electronic, photocopying, recording, videotaping, or otherwise, without the prior written permission of the publisher. No one shall upload this title, or part of this title, to any social media websites.

The right of Paul Reakes to be identified as author of this work has been asserted by him in accordance with Section 77 of the Copyright, Designs and Patents Act 1988

CHARACTERS

Dotty Dumplin, the royal cook
Prince Peski, the King's brother
Princess Pariah, his wife
The Herald
Florian, the King's aide
Old King Cole
1st Fiddler
2nd Fiddler
3rd Fiddler
Debbie, Dotty's daughter
Little King Cole
Lady Dragonia

Chorus of: **Courtiers, Pages, Townsfolk, Tradespeople** and **Creatures** of the Forbidden Forest

SYNOPSIS OF SCENES

ACT I
Scene 1 The Royal Palace of Old King Cole
Scene 2 Outside the Palace Gates
Scene 3 The Town Square
Scene 4 Outside the Palace Gates
Scene 5 The Forbidden Forest

ACT II
Scene 1 The Town Square
Scene 2 Outside the Gates
Scene 3 The Royal Palace
Scene 4 Outside the Palace Gates
Scene 5 The Forbidden Forest
Scene 6 Outside the Palace Gates
Scene 7 The Grand Finale

Time — Pantotime

MUSICAL NUMBERS

ACT I

No 1	Song and Dance	The Courtiers
No 2	Dance and Song	Pages and Fiddlers
No 3	Song and Dance	Old King Cole, Florian and Courtiers
No 4	Comedy Song	Fiddlers
No 5	Song and Dance	Townsfolk
No 6	Romantic Duet	Florian and Debbie
No 6a	Reprise of Song 6 (optional)	Florian and Debbie
No 7	Song and Dance	Dotty and Townsfolk
No 8	Song and Dance	Creatures of the Forest
No 8a	Reprise of Song 8	Creatures of the Forest

ACT II

No 9	Song and Dance	Fiddlers and Townsfolk
No 10	Comedy Evil Song and Dance	Pariah, Peski and Townsfolk
No 11	Comedy Song and Dance	Dotty and Fiddlers
No 12	Song and Dance	Pages and Courtiers
No 12a	Reprise of Song 8	Creatures of the Forest
No 13	Romantic Duet	Florian and Debbie
No 14	Song and Dance	All
No 15	House Song	Dotty, Fiddlers and the Audience
No 16	Finale Song or Reprise	All

CHARACTERS AND COSTUMES

Dotty Dumplin (Dame) is the royal cook. She is a larger-than-life "lady" of changing moods. One minute she is fun-loving and gushing, the next, she is blunt and sarcastic. But whatever her mood, you can't help liking the old girl. She is always on friendly and confidential terms with the audience and never misses an opportunity of involving them. Singing and dancing ability is an advantage with this role, but good characterization and camaraderie with the audience is essential. Needless to say, all her costumes, hair-dos and make-up are ludicrous and funny. Apart from her cook's costumes, she gets to wear an outrageous outfit with a very short skirt and platform shoes. Regal robes and a crown for the Finale.

Prince Peski (Baddie) is Old King Cole's younger brother. He is dominated by his scheming wife, and lives in fear of his awesome mother-in-law. Under these circumstances, you might be tempted to feel sorry for him. Well, don't waste your sympathy! He is a thoroughly unpleasant individual. A snivelling, cowardly weasel of a man who deserves every boo and hiss he gets! Singing and dancing ability is not essential for this role, but strong characterization is. His costume is elegant although its cut and colour should give him a sinister appearance. A regal robe for when he has made himself the King.

Princess Pariah (Baddie) is Peski's wife. She is the mastermind behind the evil plot to dispose of Old King Cole and make her husband the King. She will resort to any lengths to achieve this, even to the extent of devising exploding birthday cakes and calling on the powers of darkness! Both she and Peski never miss an opportunity of stirring the audience into a frenzy of boos and hisses. Singing and dancing ability is not essential for this role, but a strong, dominant personality certainly is. Her costume is elegant, but should give her a sinister and menacing appearance. As does her head-dress, hair-style and make-up. A regal robe and crown for when she makes herself the Queen.

The Herald (Small character part) is very much a law unto himself and he doesn't care who knows it! His duty, apart from making the occasional announcement, is to blow fanfares from his trusty trumpet. (These he mimes to sound effects played over the sound system.) No singing or dancing required. The part can be played equally well as a truculent teenager or a petulant pensioner. He wears (without too much elegance!) a tabard bearing the royal insignia, baggy tights and hat with a wilting plume.

Florian (Principal boy) is the King's aide. He is a handsome, dashing young man with great charm and gracious manners. He takes his job at the palace very seriously, and is totally loyal to Old King Cole. However, his allegiance is certainly put to the test when the King decides to marry the girl he has just fallen in love with. But duty is duty, and it seems that the lovers must part. Some strong acting is required to portray this conflict between love and duty. A good singing voice and dancing ability is needed for this role. His costumes are resplendent and show off his gorgeous pair of legs. Special Finale costume.

Old King Cole (Comedy character part) is indeed a merry old soul and much loved by all his subjects. He is also a rather naïve and foolish old soul. He is totally unaware that his evil brother and sister-in-law are plotting to get rid of him and take over the throne. He also decides that he wants to be married, and chooses the same girl who has just fallen in love with his young aide. If this wasn't bad enough, he lets the scheming Pariah persuade him to take a dip in the magic pool to regain his long lost youth. This ends in disaster when she transforms him into a ten-year-old boy! However, by the end he realizes the folly of his ways and puts things right. He even ends up marrying Dotty! This is a character part that should be made likable and endearing. For all his years he is still spry and active, if at times a little befuddled. Singing and dancing is not essential. Regal regalia and crown. White hair and beard. For his dip in the magic pool he wears long red combinations. Splendid regal robes and crown for the Finale.

The Three Fiddlers are the palace entertainers. They are very short on conversation, and when they do speak it is at the same time and mostly in words of one syllable. Their main purpose is to provide song and dance, but they are also involved in comic business with Dotty and audience participation. They can be an all male/all female trio, or a mixture of both. They use prop fiddles for their initial entrance and these can be discarded later, if so desired. They wear matching troubadour type outfits with tabards, tights and feathered caps. "Page boy" style wigs of the same colour would be a nice touch.

Debbie (Principal girl) is Dotty's daughter. This comes as a surprise because she is a pretty and petite young woman with a quiet, unassuming manner. Not a bit like her boisterous mum. She is soon beguiled by Florian, and falls hopelessly in love with him. When chosen to be Old King Cole's wife she is naturally devastated. And Florian's obsession with his royal duty doesn't help matters. Some strong emotional acting is required when this conflict comes into being. A good singing voice and dancing ability is needed for this role. Her costumes are all homespun, but they are neat and attractive. Special Finale costume.

Little King Cole (Child's part) is Old King Cole transformed into a ten-year-old boy! This is the result of his entering the magic pool and Pariah's evil trickery. Although greatly reduced in size and years, he is still very much the King. The trouble is, no one will believe him. Eventually, he convinces Dotty and together they set out to thwart the baddies by returning him to his true age. The role should be played by a competent youngster (preferably male) who has the ability to make the plight of this character believable. No singing or dancing is required. He only has one costume: a duplicate of the long red combinations as worn by Old King Cole.

Lady Dragonia (Comedy character part) is Pariah's mother and Peski's much feared mother-in-law. He has good reason to be scared because she is a very formidable old lady. But as she delights in deriding him at every opportunity we can't help liking her. Being both a battleaxe and a dabbler in the Black Arts, she is a cross between Lady Bracknell and one of the three witches! A strong, dominant personality, with mystical tendencies, is needed for this role. No singing or dancing is required. Her costume borders on the bizarre, with many baubles, bangles and beads. Her hair is a strange hue and is surmounted by a hat of peculiar design. (She only appears in Act II)

The **Chorus**, **Dancers** and **Children** appear as Courtiers, Pages, Townsfolk and Creatures of the Forbidden Forest. All participate in the action and musical numbers. There are several small speaking parts. The costumes for the Courtiers should look rich and elegant. The Pages wear tights, short tunics and small round hats. The Townsfolk should be in picturesque homespun. The Creatures of the Forbidden Forest are grotesque beings of varying shapes and sizes. Some are huge and hairy, others are small and reptilian. In other words, something to suit all age groups.

PRODUCTION NOTES

The Pantomime offers opportunities for elaborate staging, but can be produced quite simply if funds and facilities are limited.

There are three full sets:
> The Royal Palace of Old King Cole
> The Town Square
> The Forbidden Forest

These are interlinked by one front cloth:
> Outside the Palace Gates

There can be a special Finale setting, or the Royal Palace set can be used.

STAGING

The settings are fairly standard, and should not present any problems. The royal palace interior should look rich and sumptuous. There is a raised area at the back with steps leading down. On a daïs stands the royal throne. The town square is surrounded by picturesque houses and shops. Prominent is a dress shop. The rest of the town is seen in the background with a distant view of the palace. The Forbidden Forest is the classic "spooky" forest of fairy tales. Grotesquely twisted trees, crawling creepers and tangled undergrowth. To one side is the entrance to a cave in which lies a magic pool. Outside the palace gates is a front cloth used to interlink the above settings. It is painted to represent a wall with elaborate wrought-iron gates, through which can be seen the palace. If this is not practical, tabs can be used.

SPECIAL PROPS

These consist of two cakes. The first is Old King Cole's birthday cake (prop cake). It should be very large, elaborately iced and covered with lots of candles (unlit). It also has a "Happy Birthday" ribbon around it. There needs to be a duplicate ribbon for Dotty Dumplin to wear around her neck after the explosion. The cake is mounted on a trolley that can be easily pushed on and off stage. The second cake has to be big enough for the boy playing Little King Cole to be concealed inside. It can be made from light wood or strong cardboard which is then painted and decorated to resemble an enormous iced cake. It should have a removable top. This cake is also mounted on a trolley which needs to be able to sustain the weight and is safe.

LIGHTING

Bright general lighting for the palace, town square and front cloth scenes. A romantic lighting change is required for the love duets. In the Forbidden Forest scenes there is a chance for some really spooky and weird lighting effects. The shimmering reflection of water is seen at the cave entrance to show that the magic pool lies within. An eerie follow spot for Pariah as she casts her magic spell. Every time she mentions the Forbidden Forest there is a flash of lightning. Further use of follow spots for entrances, musical numbers and comic business, etc., is left to the discretion of the individual director.

EFFECTS

There is a blinding flash, a loud bang and a puff of smoke as Old King Cole's birthday cake explodes (off stage). Three more flashes are also required from inside the cave. For the Forbidden Forest scenes some carefully controlled ground mist and strange background noises will enhance the spooky atmosphere. A great clap of thunder accompanies the flash of lightning every time Pariah mentions the Forbidden Forest. An echo effect is required for those speaking from inside the cave. Also, several loud splashes are heard as characters fall or are pushed into the magic pool. Pre-recorded fanfares are needed to play over the sound system. Also a rock number and some loud dramatic music to cover Dotty's miming of the final magic spell. It would be a nice touch to hear Baby Peski and Baby Pariah bawling and crying as they are brought from the cave.

Have fun!

Paul Reakes

Other works by Paul Reakes
published by Samuel French Ltd

Pantomimes

Babes in the Wood
Bluebeard
Cinderella
Dick Turpin
Goody Two Shoes
King Arthur
King Humpty Dumpty
Little Bo Peep
Little Jack Horner
Little Miss Muffet
Little Red Riding Hood
Little Tommy Tucker
Old Mother Hubbard
Robinson Crusoe and the Pirates
Santa in Space
Sinbad the Sailor
Tom Thumb

Plays

Bang, You're Dead!
Mantrap

ACT I

Scene 1

The Royal Palace of Old King Cole

Full set. The backcloth and side wings represent a sumptuous regal interior. There is a raised area at the back with steps leading down. Up R, *there is a daïs on which stands the royal throne. Entrances* R *and* L *and at the back*

When the CURTAIN *rises, the Chorus, as Courtiers, are discovered. They go straight into the opening song and dance*

Song 1

After the number, Dotty Dumplin enters from R

Dotty (*greeting the Courtiers*) Hello, you lot! (*Spotting the audience*) Ooo! Look! We've got visitors! (*Calling to them*) Hello!

A few replies

(*To Courtiers*) Crikey! What have you done to 'em? They've dozed off already! (*To the audience, coming forward*) I said ... (*Yelling*) HELLO!!

The audience yells back

That's better. That's more like it. Well, it's lovely to see you all and I'm Dotty. (*To someone*) No, that's my *name,* dear, not my condition. Dotty Dumplin, that's me. Cook to his Majesty, Old King Cole. I'm a sort of Nigella Lawson with royal icing. Cake making is my speciality. I make cakes for all the special occasions here at the palace. And today's *really* special because it's Old King Cole's birthday. I've made him a lovely big cake. The only trouble is, there's so many candles you can hardly see the cake. He's ever so old, y'see. How old do you think he is? (*Ad-lib with the audience*) No, you're all wrong. And I'm not gonna tell you because it's classified inflammation. Oh, but he's a lovely chap, is dear Old King Cole. Not a bit like that nasty brother of his.

Unseen by her, sinister Prince Peski enters from L

Prince Peski, that's his name. Peski by name and pesky by nature. You'd never think they were brothers. Oh, he's really *horrible!*

The equally sinister Princess Pariah enters from L, *and joins Peski*

And so's that wife of his! Princess Pariah! She's a right horror too. The pair of 'em would give Dracula nightmares.

On seeing the sinister couple, the Courtiers make hasty exits in various directions

The pair move down on either side of the unsuspecting Dotty. The audience will probably be shouting out warnings, but she takes no notice

Most people are scared stiff of 'em, y'know. But not me. Oh, no! If they were here now, I'd give 'em a right ear-bashin'. I'd tell that pair just what I thought of 'em. D'you know what I'd say?
Peski No. What would you say?

Dotty becomes aware of them and reacts

Dotty (*to the audience*) It's *them!* You could have warned me! (*To them, with a sickly grin*) Mornin'... Mornin'.
Pariah Well? What are you going to say?
Dotty (*gulping*) I ... I was gonna say ... what a lovely year it is for the time of weather.
Peski Wasn't it something about giving us an ear-bashing?
Dotty What? Oh, no! I said *smashing!* I think you're both *smashing!*
Pariah It didn't sound like that.
Dotty Well, it's these new teeth. I have trouble pronouncing my worms. See, there I go again.
Peski Come on! *Out with it!*
Dotty What 'ere? In front of all these people?!
Pariah Would you like to pay a little visit to the torture chamber?
Dotty No thanks. I went before I came.
Peski How do you fancy being boiled in oil?
Dotty Would that be nut-free oil? Only I'm allergic to nuts. Present company accepted, of course.

Pariah How would you like to be stretched on the rack?
Dotty I don't mind. A few more inches and I'd be just like [current model]
Peski Enough of this! What were you going to say to us!
Pariah And if you don't tell us, you will be made to suffer all manner of excruciating tortures!
Dotty (*with false bravado*) You can't scare me! I'm imperious to pain. I've been to [local place]!
Peski }
Pariah } (*together, snarling at her*) *Tell us!!*
Dotty All right! Don't get yer knickers in a knot. I'll tell you what I was going to say. I think you two are —
Peski }
Pariah } (*together, threateningly*) Yes?!
Dotty I think you are just like a pair of angels that fell from the sky.
Peski }
Pariah } (*very flattered*) Oh, how nice.
Dotty Yes, isn't it. What a pity you both landed on yer face!

Dotty runs out at the nearest exit

Peski (*enraged*) What! (*He makes to pursue Dotty*) Come back here!
Pariah (*stopping him*) Wait, Peski! Don't demean yourself. She's not worth it.
Peski You're right, my little wasp. (*With evil relish*) I can wait.
Pariah Yes. As soon as you become king you can make her suffer. You can make them *all* suffer!
Peski (*indicating the audience*) And that applies to *this* rabble, as well. Who are these parasites, by the way?
Pariah I don't know. (*Peering at them*) They don't look very nice, do they?
Peski Absolutely abominable! (*He sniffs*) They don't *smell* very nice either.
Pariah Positively putrid!
Peski When I'm king this lot will be the first to go. (*To audience*) Oh, yes, you will!
Audience Oh, no, we won't!
Peski }
Pariah } (*together*) Oh, yes, you will!
Audience Oh, no, we won't!

This continues ad-lib

Peski (*petulantly*) We keep talking about when I become King, but how much longer am I to wait?
Pariah As soon as your ridiculous old brother is out of the way the throne will be yours, my dear.
Peski But we've tried all ways to get rid of him! None of them have worked.
Pariah Today's plan will work, I assure you.
Peski Hah! You've said that before! What is it this time? More poison? The last time we tried that, *I* drank it by mistake and couldn't leave the bathroom for a week! Or is it to be another so-called fatal accident? Like the time he was supposed to fall into the moat and drown. What happened? I tripped over him and fell in myself! I'm still finding tadpoles in places where tadpoles shouldn't be! (*He wiggles his leg*)
Pariah Have faith, Peski. My plan is perfect. It will not fail.
Peski What is it?
Pariah A birthday cake! The last birthday cake Old King Cole will ever see.
Peski (*sneering*) Are you hoping he'll die from indigestion?
Pariah It is a specially prepared cake. I have just substituted it for the one Dotty Dumplin has made for him. She will never know the difference. It looks exactly like hers except for one very special ingredient.
Peski And what's that?
Pariah (*with evil relish*) An explosive device! As soon as King Cole cuts the first slice — *BANG!!* No more Old King Cole!
Peski }
Pariah } (*together, indulging in fiendish laughter*) Hee! Hee! Hee!
Pariah And the beauty of it is, no suspicion can fall on us. That stupid cook will get the blame. There must have been something terribly wrong with her cake mixture.
Peski Ingenious! Truly ingenious! My brother's last birthday will certainly go with a bang! Oh! You're very clever, my little puff adder. (*He kisses her on the cheek*)
Pariah (*snapping at him*) What do you think you are doing, Peski?! You know you must give a week's notice before you can kiss me!
Peski I'm sorry, my dear. I got excited. You're so clever! (*To the audience*) Isn't she clever?
Audience No!
Pariah Oh, yes, I am!
Audience Oh, no, you're not!

This continues ad-lib

Peski Well, we don't care what *you* think!
Pariah No, you're just a pile of insignificant rubbish!

Act I, Scene 1   5

Sneering and snarling at the audience, they exit L

The Herald enters at the back. He blows a fanfare on his trumpet

Fanfare sounds

The Courtiers rush on and fill the sides. Handsome young Florian, the King's aide, enters on the raised area at the back

Florian Attention! Your attention, please! His royal majesty King Cole will be here at any moment. As you know, today is his birthday, so prepare to greet him with a rousing chorus of "Happy Birthday to You". (*Looking off*) Here he comes now! Get ready!

The Herald blows another fanfare. Fanfare sounds

Old King Cole enters on the raised area

Florian and the others sing "Happy Birthday Dear Kingy". King Cole comes down the steps, followed by Florian

King Cole Thank you, my friends. Thank you, one and all. (*Catching sight of the audience and turning to Florian*) I say, Florian. Who are these good folk?

They move down to take a closer look

I don't recognize them. Do you?
Florian No, Your Majesty. I shall attempt to converse with them.
King Cole Hadn't you better try talking to them first? (*He chuckles at his "joke"*)
Florian (*to the audience*) Hello! How do you do.
Audience Hello!
Florian They seem nice enough, Your Majesty.
King Cole Yes, they do. (*To the audience*) Greetings!
Audience Greetings!
King Cole Are you from a part of my kingdom?
Audience No.
King Cole Where are you from then?

The audience calls out various place names

(*To Florian*) Where did they say? I didn't catch a word of that.

Florian I think you'll have to ask them individually, Your Majesty.
King Cole Jolly good idea. (*To someone*) Hello. Would *you* like to tell me where you come from, please.

Name of a local place is given

Oh, dear. Well, it can't be helped. Someone has to live there. (*To someone else*) Hello. And where do you come from?

Name of another place is given

Oh, I went there once. But it was closed! (*To all*) Well, wherever you come from, you're all very welcome. Especially today, because it's my birthday. Isn't that right, Florian?
Florian Indeed it is, Your Majesty. (*To the audience*) You're all very welcome.
King Cole (*to the audience, indicating Florian*) Nice lad, isn't he? Lovely manners. And the best pair of legs this side of [local place]!

King Cole and the Courtiers roar with laughter

The laughter soon dies as Peski and Pariah enter from L

King Cole Oh, dear! Here come the wet blankets!
Peski (*with a smarmy bow*) Greetings, brother.
King Cole Hello, Peski.
Pariah (*with a smarmy curtsey*) Greetings, Your Majesty.
King Cole Hello, sister-in-law.
Peski May we both be permitted to wish you a very happy birthday.
King Cole Thank you.
Peski We haven't brought you our present yet.
Pariah No, it will be arriving shortly.

They cackle together

King Cole (*to the audience*) I know he's my brother, but he gives my goose pimples goose pimples.
Peski (*looking about*) Surely there is something missing.
King Cole Missing? What?
Pariah Why, yes. Your birthday cake!
King Cole By Jove, you're right! A birthday wouldn't be a birthday without a cake. Florian, have my cake brought in.
Florian (*with a bow*) At once, Your Majesty.

Act I, Scene 1　　　　　　　　　　　　　　　　　　　　　　　　7

King Cole No, wait! Not yet. We're forgetting the daily ceremony. We must attend to that first. (*He sits on his throne*)

Peski and Pariah show their annoyance

(*To the audience*) Allow me to explain. A few years ago someone made up a rhyme about me. Oh, not *that* sort of rhyme. (*He chuckles*) No, this is a clean one. It's become a tradition that every day at this time I repeat the rhyme, and then we have a little ceremony. It's a very jolly rhyme, and goes like this. (*He clears his throat and recites the rhyme*)
>Old King Cole is a merry old soul,
>A merry old soul is he.
>He calls for his pipe,
>He calls for his bowl,
>And he calls for his Fiddlers three!

Song 2

To suitable music, two Pages enter. One is carrying a long clay pipe on a cushion. The other, a large punch bowl. They perform a dance sequence

When it ends, the Pages clear to one side

The music changes, and the three Fiddlers make their entrance. They carry prop fiddles. They bow to the King

Fiddlers Happy birthday, Your Majesty!
King Cole Thank you, Fiddlers. One, two, three.
Fiddlers　　　　We have prepared for this special day,
　　　　　　　　A treat that will take your breath away.
　　　　　　　　So now, without any further ado,
　　　　　　　　Here is our birthday gift to you!

The Fiddlers perform their number. At the end, the King and the others applaud

King Cole (*to the audience*) Now, that's what I call the X Factor (*or current fad*).
Peski (*impatiently*) Yes, yes, very nice. Now it's time for your birthday cake, brother.
King Cole Ah, yes! My cake! I'm really looking forward to that.

Peski }
Pariah } (*together, to the audience*) So are we!
King Cole (*to Florian*) Be so good as to summon the royal cook.
Florian (*calling to off stage*) Summon the royal cook!
Courtiers (*doing the same*) Summon the royal cook!
Voice (*off stage, calling*) Summon the royal cook!
Voice (*further off stage, calling*) Summon the royal cook!

Dotty pops her head out from R

Dotty Did somebody somewhere summon a summon? (*Business with teeth*) Cor! I nearly lost me top set!
King Cole Hello, Dotty!
Dotty (*going to him*) Oh! Hello, Yer Majfulness! Many happy returns of the day. May I say, you don't look a day older! If I had sore eyes you'd be a sight for 'em! And may I also say —
Peski You may *not!*
Pariah Be silent, crone!
Dotty 'Ere! It's *Mrs* Crone to you!
Peski Don't be insolent, woman!
Dotty Who are you callin' a woman! I'll 'ave you know, I've rubbed shoulders with [local dignitary]!
Peski Enough of this! His Majesty is waiting for his birthday cake.
Dotty (*gushing*) Oh, yes! The cake! It's all ready! An' it's a real cracker this year too, Yer Maj. I've excelled myself! I've put my heart and soul into it!
King Cole That doesn't sound very appetizing!
Dotty Eh? (*Then realizing he is joking*) Oh! You are a one!
Pariah Don't keep His Majesty waiting! Bring in the cake!
Dotty Stop orderin' me about! Who do you think *you* are — [current or local reference]?
King Cole Please will you bring in my cake, Dotty?
Dotty (*sweetly*) Of course I will, Your Royal Flush. (*Pointedly*) If *you* say so.

She pokes her tongue out at Peski and Pariah, and then exits R

Pariah That woman! She needs taking down a peg!
Peski She needs taking down to the rubbish tip, if you ask me!

Dotty enters from R. *She is pushing a trolley. On it is a large birthday cake decorated with icing, lots of candles and a "Happy Birthday" ribbon*

Act I, Scene 1   9

Unseen by the others, Peski and Pariah rub their hands in devilish glee. As she pushes the cake to centre, Dotty sings "Happy birthday, dear Kingy". King Cole leaves his throne to admire the cake

Dotty There it is! All made by my own fair 'and! Well, what d'you think of it?
King Cole Splendid, Dotty. Absolutely splendid.
Dotty Ta! It's my piece of resistance. I thought it'd go down a bomb.

Peski and Pariah are hard put to suppress their evil chuckles

King Cole (*to them*) What's wrong?
Peski (*recovering*) Er ... nothing, brother. It's a magnificent-looking cake.
Pariah I hope it tastes as good as it looks.
Dotty (*indignantly*) Course it does!
Peski Hurry up and cut the first slice, brother. Then we can all try some.
Dotty (*handing him a knife from the trolley*) Here yah go, Yer Maj.

Peski and Pariah quickly move away to down L. *They crouch together and put their fingers in their ears. King Cole is about to cut into the cake, when Dotty gives a yell*

Whoa! Wait, Your Maj!
King Cole What's the matter?
Dotty I've forgotten to light the candles. You won't be able to make a wish. What *am* I like! I'd forget me head if it wasn't screwed on! I'll take it back it to the kitchen and light 'em right away! Won't take a minute! Mind yer backs!

Dotty pushes the trolley out R

Peski and Pariah are still crouched with their fingers in their ears. The others become aware of this and look at them with curiosity. A pause. Eventually, Pariah takes her fingers from her ears

Pariah (*to Peski, in a stage whisper*) Has it gone off? Peski? (*He still has his fingers in his ears*) Peski! (*She bellows at him*) PESKI!!
Peski (*jumping with fright*) Yahh! What?
Pariah (*in a stage whisper*) Has it gone off?

King Cole moves down to beside Peski

Peski (*in a stage whisper*) I don't know.
Pariah (*in a stage whisper*) I didn't hear anything.
Peski (*in a stage whisper*) Neither did I. (*To King*) Did *you* hear anything? (*He reacts at seeing the King*) Ahh! You're still here!
King Cole Of course I am.
Pariah (*looking about*) Where's the cake?
King Cole Dotty forgot to light the candles. She's doing it now.

There is a blinding flash and a loud explosion off stage R. *If possible, smoke billows out. All react*

Dotty staggers on from R. *Her hair is standing on end and her face and upper half is covered with the exploded cake and candles. The cake ribbon hangs around her neck. She is shocked and disorientated to say the least!*

The King and Florian rush to her assistance

Dotty Ooooh! ... *Where* am I? ... *Who* am I? ... Oooh!
King Cole Dotty!
Florian What happened?
Dotty I ... I dunno! I lit the candles, and had to stand well back because of the heat. It's a good job I did, because the next thing ... *BOOM!* The whole thing blew up! There was cake and candles everywhere. It's made a right mess of my kitchen too. Y'know that great big window I've always wanted? Well, I've got it now! Oh! I've heard of endin' up with egg on yer face, but this is ridiculous! (*She wipes off some cake and licks her finger*) Mmm! It tastes smashin' too. (*She holds her finger out to King*) Have a lick.
Peski
Pariah } (*to the audience, fuming with rage*) Curses! Foiled again!

Peski and Pariah exit L

Dotty (*getting tearful*) Oh, Yer Maj! Your lovely birthday cake! All blown to smithereens! I just don't know how it happened! I used one of Delia's recipes too! I'm sorry! (*Starting to wail*) Waaah!
King Cole (*comforting her*) Now, now. Don't upset yourself.
Dotty There isn't time to bake you another one. I'll just have to go down to [local bakery] and buy one. This sort of thing would never 'appen to Gordon Ramsay! But if it did, you can bet he'd have a word for it!

Act I, Scene 1   11

Dotty makes a tearful exit R

Florian Why should a cake explode like that? It's very curious, Your Majesty.

King Cole Yes, indeed ... but never mind about that now. I have a very important announcement to make. (*Addressing the whole ensemble*) As you all know, I have been a bachelor for many, many years. Well, after much thought and serious contemplation I have come to a decision. I am going to get married!

Consternation from the others

Florian Your Majesty! This *is* a surprise. Congratulations!
Others Congratulations, Your Majesty!
King Cole Thank you. Thank you.
Florian May we be permitted to know her name?
King Cole Whose name?
Florian The lucky lady.
King Cole (*casually*) Oh, I don't know her name. I haven't met her yet.
Florian (*greatly puzzled*) You haven't met ...? I don't understand ...
King Cole It's quite simple. As I've decided to get married the obvious thing to do is find a suitable bride, is it not?
Florian Yes, Your Majesty, but ——
King Cole That will be your next job, Florian. I want you to send out a royal decree at once. All prospective brides are to present themselves at the palace this afternoon for my inspection. From them I will choose a wife. Better make it three o'clock. I don't want to miss [midday TV programme].
Florian But, Your Majesty ——
King Cole What's the matter, my boy? Don't you think it's a good idea?
Florian Well, it's not for me to question Your Majesty's decision, but ——
King Cole Exactly. And who knows, I may find true love. You wouldn't begrudge an old man that, would you?
Florian Of course not, Your Majesty.
King Cole And you know what they say ... It's never too late to fall in love!

Song 3

A lively song and dance for King Cole, Florian and the others. At the end of the number the Lights fade to black-out

Music to cover the scene change, and then the Lights come up on —

Scene 2

Outside the Palace Gates

Tabs, or front cloth showing a wall with wrought-iron gates, through which can be seen the palace. Entrances DR *and* DL

Peski enters from DL. *He is met with a barrage of abuse from the audience*

Peski (*snarling at them*) Grrr! And the same to you! Why don't you all go for a *long* walk — off a *short* pier! Ha! Ha! Ha!

Pariah, in an agitated state, rushes on from DL

Pariah Peski!
Peski Ah! My little scorpion's tail. I was just getting the better of these pathetic peasants.
Pariah Never mind that. Have you heard the awful news?
Peski It's not the [local reference] in trouble again, is it?
Pariah Worse than that. The King is intending to get married!
Peski *What!*
Pariah He's going to choose a wife at three o'clock this afternoon. He could be married before the day is out! You know what that means, don't you?
Peski A trip to Poundland for a wedding present?
Pariah No! If he marries, what will his wife become?
Peski Er ... bored?
Pariah (*exasperated*) Oh, use your brains, Peski! She will become his *queen!* Even if we manage to dispose of him, *she* will carry on ruling in his place!
Peski Oh, no!
Pariah And worse still! There might be (*with great revulsion*) *children!* Horrid little princes or princesses! All ready to take over the throne.
Peski But we can't let that happen! (*Having a childish tantrum and wailing*) *I wanna be the King!!*
Pariah (*comforting him*) There, there. I know you do, my love. And you will be. Just leave it to your little Pariah.
Peski (*after sniffing and wiping his nose on her sleeve*) What are we going to do?

Act I, Scene 2   13

Pariah His disposal is now even more urgent. We must get rid of King Cole before he has a chance to find a wife and make her his queen.
Peski But how? We've only got until three o' clock!
Pariah I don't know yet. But, never fear. *I* will think of something! (*To the audience*) Oh, yes, I will!
Audience Oh, no, you won't!
Peski
Pariah } (*together*) Oh, yes, I/she will!

After a routine with audience, Peski and Pariah exit DL

Dotty enters from DR. *She has cleaned herself up and is carrying a cake box*

Dotty (*greeting the audience*) Hello, folks! Well, I've been down to [local bakers] to buy King Cole a birthday cake, and guess what? They've sold out! Typical! All they had left are these. Four cream cakes.

The Fiddlers enter from DR

Fiddlers Hello, Dotty!
Dotty Oh! It's the three tiddlers!
Fiddlers (*correcting her*) *Fiddlers!*
Dotty Think yourselves lucky I didn't say what I first thought of!
Fiddlers What's in the box?
Dotty Four cream cakes.
Fiddlers (*moving in, licking their lips*) Mmm! Cream cakes!
Dotty (*holding the box away from them*) Ger off! These are for Old King Cole to replace his busted birthday cake.
Fiddlers (*showing disapproval*) Huh!
Dotty What d'you mean — Huh? Don't you think they're good enough?
Fiddlers (*shaking their heads*) No!
Dotty I suppose you're right. It's not the same as a birthday cake, is it? What shall I do with them?

The Fiddlers look hopeful

Dotty Oh, well! Waste not, want not, that's my grotto. I'll just have to eat 'em meself!
Fiddlers *All* of them?!
Dotty That's the idea.

Fiddlers Greedy!
Dotty I suppose you think I should share them with you?
Fiddlers Yes.
Dotty (*to the audience*) Shall I?
Audience ⎫ (*together*) Yes!
Fiddlers ⎭
Dotty Are you sure?
Audience ⎫ (*together*) Yes!
Fiddlers ⎭
Dotty Are you really, *really* sure?
Audience ⎫ (*together*) Yes!
Fiddlers ⎭
Dotty Well, I'm not goin' to! *I* paid for 'em, so *I'm* gonna eat 'em! So there! (*She opens the box and gloats over the cakes*)

The Fiddlers get into a huddle

(*Licking her lips*) Mmmm! Don't they look yummy! Now, which one shall I eat first?

As she is making her selection, the Fiddlers gather around her and peer into the box

Fiddlers Ugh!!
Dotty What's wrong?
Fiddlers There's a fly!
Dotty A fly? (*Looking in the box*) Where? I can't see it.
Fiddlers Look closer!
Dotty (*doing so*) I can't see any fly!
Fiddlers Look closer!
Dotty (*doing so, her nose nearly in the box*) No! I still can't see it!

The Fiddlers grin to the audience

Fiddlers (*to the audience*) Shall we?
Audience Yes!
Fiddlers (*putting their thumbs up*) Right! One! Two! *Three!*

They push the box up into Dotty's face. She emerges with a cake- (crazy foam-) covered face. The Fiddlers roar with laughter

Dotty Oh, no! I'm plastered again! I suppose I had that comin' for being so greedy.

Act I, Scene 3   15

Fiddlers Yes!
Dotty (*to the audience*) You could say I got my just — *desserts!*

Dotty stumbles out DL

Song 4

A song for the Fiddlers

At the end, they troop off DR, *waving to the audience*

The Lights fade to black-out. Music to cover the scene change, and then the Lights come up on —

SCENE 3

The Town Square

Full set. The side wings represent picturesque houses and shops. Predominant is a dress shop. The backcloth shows the rest of the town with the royal palace in the distance. Entrances R *and* L, *and at the back*

Music. The Chorus and Dancers, as Townsfolk, are discovered going about their business. This develops into a song and dance routine

Song 5

After the number, the Herald enters at the back with his trumpet

The Townsfolk clear to the sides. The Herald blows his trumpet. Fanfare sounds

Florian enters at the back and moves to C

Florian (*announcing to the ensemble*) All loyal subjects of the crown pay heed to this royal decree. His most gracious Majesty, King Cole, wishes it to be known throughout the land that he has decided to enter the state of connubial bliss.
Townsfolk (*not understanding*) Where?
Florian He wants to get married.
Townsfolk Oh! (*Reacting*) What!

Constanternation from the crowd

Florian Silence! In consequence of this, all prospective brides are invited to present themselves at the royal palace this afternoon at three o'clock. His Majesty will conduct an interview with each candidate. From these he will choose his bride-to-be and future queen. That is the end of this special announcement. (*He turns away to confer with the Herald*)
1st Male Cor! Old King Cole getting wed!
2nd Male He must be mad!
1st Female I wish I was single so that I could have a go!
2nd Male (*obviously her husband*) So do I!
2nd Female (*preening herself*) D'you think he'll pick me?
3rd Female Not if I get there first!

Full of excitement, the Townsfolk rush out in various directions. At the same time, pretty young Debbie Dumplin enters from R

Debbie Good heavens! What's happening?
2nd Female (*pointing to Florian*) Ask *him!* I've got to get down to [local beauty/hair salon]!

2nd Female exits

Debbie (*approaching Florian, a little nervously*) Er ... excuse me.
Florian Yes? (*He turns and obviously likes what he sees*) Oh, hello!
Debbie Hello. Please can you tell me something?
Florian With pleasure. My name is Florian. I'm aide to His Majesty the King. I live at the palace. Blue (*or whatever the colour of her costume*) is my favourite colour and Wednesday is my day off.
Debbie (*smiling*) Thank you. That's very informative. But I meant what's all the excitement about?
Florian Oh, that. Well, I've just announced that King Cole wants to get married. He's hoping to pick himself a wife this afternoon.
Debbie (*incredulously*) *Pick* a wife? You mean someone he doesn't even know?
Florian That's the idea.
Debbie That doesn't seem right. I thought you had to fall in love with someone before you asked them to marry you. But perhaps I'm being old-fashioned.
Florian Oh, I don't think you're old-fashioned at all. I think you're very ... very new-fashioned. Every bit of you.
Debbie Well ... Thank you for telling me. Goodbye. (*She moves to exit* R)

Act I, Scene 3   17

Florian Wait! Just a minute. I ... er ... (*To the Herald*) You can go.
Herald Wot?
Florian I said you can go. (*Propelling him towards exit* L) Make your way to [local] Street. I'll catch up with you when I've ... er ... (*He looks towards Debbie*)
Herald (*nudging Florian*) Oh, I get yah! (*He gives a knowing wink*) Best o' luck!

Herald exits L

Florian (*moving back to Debbie*) Sorry about that. Now, what did you say your name was?
Debbie (*smiling*) I didn't. It's Debbie. Short for Deborah.
Florian Charming.
Debbie Debbie Dumplin.
Florian (*reacting*) I say!
Debbie I know. It's not very flattering, is it?
Florian No ... I mean I know another Dumplin. She's ——
Debbie My mother. Dotty Dumplin. She's the cook at the palace.
Florian Good heavens! So you're Dotty's daughter. Well, all I can say is your father must have been very beautiful.
Debbie (*smiling*) Are you saying my mother isn't?
Florian (*hastily*) Perhaps we should change the subject. I quite agree with what you said just now.
Debbie What was that?
Florian About falling in love. (*After a slight pause*) Are *you* in love with anybody, Debbie?
Debbie Yes.
Florian (*disappointed*) Oh! Who's the lucky chap?
Debbie My mother.
Florian (*brightening*) Ah! That's a different sort of love. The kind of love I'm talking about is ... is ...
Debbie Yes?
Florian Let me try to explain.

Song 6

Romantic duet and dance with romantic lighting change. After the number the lighting returns to normal

Florian Now do you understand what I mean by love?
Debbie (*gazing at him, breathlessly*) Oh, yes.
Florian And do you feel that way about me?

Debbie (*as before*) Oh, yes.
Florian That's good. Because I certainly feel that way about you.
Debbie Florian!
Florian Debbie!

They embrace

> I must go now. I have my royal duties to attend to. But I promise I'll return as soon as I can. Until then ... (*He embraces her*) *Au revoir*!

He goes to exit L, *turns to blow her a kiss and then goes*

On cloud nine, Debbie waltzes around, humming the refrain of the duet

Dotty (*off* R, *calling*) Debbie! Deb! Where are yah! Debbie!

Dotty rushes on from R, *in a very excited state*

> Oh, there you are! You'll never guess! *You'll never guess!*

Debbie (*having come down to earth*) Guess what, Mum?
Dotty Old King Cole is gonna get married!
Debbie Yes, I know.
Dotty He's gonna choose a wife this afternoon! Excitin' init?
Debbie I suppose so.
Dotty Well, don't sound so enthuselastic, girl. I think it's great news! (*Indicating the audience*) *They* think it's great news! (*To the audience*) Don't yah, folks?
Audience Yes!
Dotty (*to Debbie*) See! Oh, perhaps you've not been introduced. (*To the audience*) This is my daughter, Debbie. Say hello to the nice people, Debbie. They won't bite. I think most of 'em have left their teeth at home.
Debbie (*waving to the audience*) Hello!
Audience Hello!
Dotty (*to the audience*) Oh, I know what you're all thinking. You don't think I look old enough to be her mother, do yah?

By-play with the audience

> All right, all right! There's no need to take a vote on it!

Debbie (*eager to tell her news*) Mum, I've got something to tell you.
Dotty (*not listening and prattling on, excitedly*) Now, it's at three o'clock, so I'll have to get me skates on. I'll need to get down to

Act I, Scene 3

[local beauty/hair salon] for a makeover. There's bound to be a mad stampede for the paint and Polyfilla. I'll be needin' a new outfit too. Come on, you can help me pick something out. (*She makes for the dress shop*)

Debbie Mum, calm down. What are you talking about?

Dotty He's bound to pick me. I've got the advantage over all the others. I've been doin' his cookin' for years! And he loves my grub. Especially when I give him a Spotted Dick. And you know the old sayin'. The way to a man's heart is through his cake 'ole.

Debbie Mum, you're not seriously thinking of putting yourself forward as the King's bride, are you?

Dotty And why not? He's a lonely old bachelor and I'm a lonely old ... er ... *youngish* widow. We're perfectly combatable.

Debbie But, Mum —

Dotty But nothing! I'll make a lovely queen. Look! (*Showing off her profile*) I've got just the right sort of face for a stamp.

Debbie Mum —

Dotty Oh, I know he's years older than me, but it's amazing what a couple of cans of Red Bull can do.

Debbie Mum —

Dotty I must say you're not being very supportive, Debbie. Don't you think I've got a chance?

Debbie Of course I do. I don't want you to be disappointed, that's all. He's going to have lots of others to choose from, you know. Lots of ... er ... *younger* ones.

Dotty Huh! And all of 'em nitwits and brainless bimbos! What he needs is a woman with a good head on 'er shoulders. And heads don't come much gooder than mine. Oh, I'm wastin' time 'ere! (*To the audience*) Bye, folks! The next time you see me I'll be transformed into a second [current female personality]!

She rushes into the dress shop

Debbie Mum! (*She is about to follow Dotty into the shop*)

Florian enters from R

Florian (*moving to her*) Debbie! I'm back as promised. Now, where did we get to? Ah, yes. I remember. (*He takes her in his arms*)

King Cole (*off* R, *calling*) Florian? *Florian?*

Florian (*breaking away from Debbie*) It's the King!

King Cole enters from R. *Debbie remains partially hidden behind Florian*

King Cole Ah! There you are. I just wanted to know how things are progressing. Have you informed the populace?
Florian Yes, Your Majesty.
King Cole Good. And what's the response from the ladies?
Florian Very favourable, sire. I think you will have a large selection to choose from.
King Cole Capital! But not *too* large, I hope. I want to get it all sorted out before *Eggheads*, and —— (*Suddenly becoming aware of Debbie*) But, who's that you're hiding?
Florian Oh, I'm sorry, Your Majesty. Allow me to present Miss Dumplin. (*He steps back to reveal Debbie fully to the King*)
Debbie (*curtsying*) Your Majesty. (*Then with a charming smile*) May I be permitted to wish you a very happy birthday.

King Cole is awestruck at the sight of Debbie. He just gapes at her. Eventually, he pulls himself together, and takes Florian away to one side

King Cole Did you say she was a Dumplin?
Florian Yes, Your Majesty. She is Dotty Dumplin's daughter.
King Cole Really? That's absolutely amazing!
Florian That's what I thought, sire.
King Cole Well, it can't be helped. She's the one!
Florian I beg your pardon?
King Cole She's the one. She's the one I want to make my wife!
Florian (*unable to believe his ears*) Your wife! But ——
King Cole She's just what I'm looking for. Pretty, charming and obviously intelligent. Yes, she's the one. So there's no point going through all that rigmarole this afternoon. You'll have to announce that it's been cancelled. I've made my choice. Now, we'll just get the formalities over with.

Florian is speechless. The King crosses to Debbie

Miss Dumplin ... I trust you have a first name.
Debbie It's Debbie. Short for Deborah, Your Majesty.
King Cole Oh, I think we can dispense with the "Your Majesties" under the circumstances. Call me Cole.
Debbie (*greatly puzzled*) Cole?
King Cole To begin with. (*Chuckling*) Whatever little pet names you choose to call me can come later.
Debbie (*even more puzzled*) I ... I'm afraid I don't understand, Your Majesty.
King Cole What? Oh, sorry. Didn't I say? I've chosen *you* to be my wife.

Act I, Scene 3　　　　　　　　　　　　　　　　　　　　　　　　　　21

Debbie is dumbfounded, to say the least!

What d'you think of that? Ah! Speechless with joy, eh? Well, I'll give you time to collect your things and say your goodbyes, and then Florian will escort you to the palace. Then we can discuss the wedding date. Well, goodbye for now. (*He moves to exit* R, *and then stops*) Oh! I almost forgot. (*He goes back to Debbie*) Congratulations, my dear. (*He gives her a peck on the cheek*) I'm sure we'll be very happy together. (*He moves to the exit* R, *and pauses to speak to the audience*) Not a very talkative girl. Still, you can't have everything.

King Cole exits

As soon as he is out of sight, Debbie and Florian rush into each other's arms

Debbie Oh, Florian! What are we going to do? I can't marry *him*. It's *you* I love!
Florian I know. And I love you, but ... but he *is* the King and his will is absolute.
Debbie What are you saying?
Florian (*sadly*) It's hopeless, Debbie. I'm afraid there can never be any future for us now.
Debbie No! Don't say that. There must be something we can do. What if we go to him and tell him how we feel about each other?
Florian It won't do any good. He's chosen you. If only we'd met before he had this idea of marrying. He's a very decent old chap, but when he's made his mind up there's no changing him.
Debbie We could run away together. Far away.
Florian And eventually he would find us. What would happen then? He'd never forgive us for defying him. We could end up being imprisoned. Or worse! There is nothing to be done. I will resign my post and leave the kingdom. You will never have to see me again.
Debbie No!
Florian It's for the best. If I remain here it will only be a constant reminder of what we have lost.
Debbie (*in tears*) Oh, Florian!

Reprise of Song 6 (Optional)

Romantic lighting if reprise is used, and then return to previous setting

The lovers clear to DR

Dotty comes out of the dress shop. She is now wearing an outrageous outfit. Very short skirt, plunging neckline and platform shoes. She has also acquired a devastating wig

The Townsfolk enter from various directions, and view Dotty's outfit with undisguised hilarity

Dotty (*showing off the outfit*) Well! What d'you think, eh? What d'you think? (*She does a twirl*) Am I stunnin' or what?
1st Male Definitely a *what!*
1st Female I thought Halloween was over, Dotty.

The Townsfolk laugh

Dotty Oh, you lot! You've got no taste. This is the latest thing! It's called the Bingo look.
2nd Male Why?
Dotty (*pulling down the neckline*) Eyes down for a full house! (*To the audience*) What do *you* think of the outfit, folks? (*She parades up and down. To someone*) I can see *you* like it, young man! Put yer tongue back in!

By-play and ad-lib with members of the audience

Well, it's done wonders for me. It's cured my furniture problem. And what's that, I hear you ask? Well, it's stopped my *chest* falling into my drawers! (*She sees Debbie and crosses to her*) Well, Deb? (*Posing*) What do you think of yer mummy now?

Debbie bursts into tears

(*To the audience*) Jealously. It's a terrible thing. (*To the others*) Old King Cole won't be able to resist me in this outfit. He'll have me up the aisle faster than the speed of light ale. So you no-hopers might as well give up right now.
Florian I'm afraid that also applies to you, Dotty.
Dotty Eh?
Florian (*to all*) Listen, all of you. This afternoon's event at the palace has been cancelled. The King has already chosen his wife-to-be.

Reaction from the others

Dotty What?! And I've just blown next month's housekeeping on makin' meself look gorgeous! Who is she?

Act I, Scene 4   23

Debbie (*after a slight pause, far from happy about it*) Me!
Dotty (*agog*) You?! Well, knock me down and fan me with a dishcloth! Oh, well! Let the best man win, I say. Come 'ere! (*She hugs Debbie*) Congratulations, luvvy! You must be over the moon.

More tears from Debbie

> (*To the audience*) Tch! Flippin' kids! There's no pleasing 'em, is there? (*To Debbie*) When's the wedding gonna be? I 'ope I can trade this lot in for a big 'at?

Florian (*to Debbie, sadly*) I think it's time we were leaving for the palace.
Dotty Oh, yes! Don't keep yer future hubby waitin'.
Debbie (*to Florian, tearfully*) I'm ... I'm ready.

Florian and Debbie make a very sad and forlorn exit R

Dotty (*to the audience*) I dunno! Youngsters these days. They're never grateful, are they? In my day we were 'appy with just a lump of coal to chew on. Anyway, *I'm* happy! My little Debbie, marryin' a king! Oh! Just think! I'll be Old King Cole's mother-in-law! Hey! That'll make me royalty too! Ha! Ha! That'll be one in the eye for the ladies of the [local] WI! Oh, I'm so happy, d'you know what I feel like doin'?

By-play with audience

> No, you mucky so-and-so! I feel like *singin'*!

Song 7

A lively song and dance for Dotty and the Townsfolk. It ends with a tableau and the Lights fade to black-out

Music to cover the scene change, and then the Lights come up on —

Scene 4

Outside the Palace Gates

As Act I, Scene 2

Pariah enters from DL. *She is reading a large book of ancient design. Peski follows her on. They are met with the usual abuse from the audience*

Pariah (*snarling at them*) Oh, do be quiet, you little pests! Can't you see I'm reading!
Peski (*to the audience*) And unlike *you,* she *can* read! Nah! (*To Pariah*) What *is* it you're reading, my little tarantula? You've had your nose stuck in that book for ages. Is it the latest [political] manifesto?
Pariah This book contains all the secrets of the black arts and sorcery.
Peski I was right then.
Pariah It belongs to my dear mother.
Peski That figures! (*Aside*) The old witch!
Pariah Pardon?
Peski (*hastily*) *Which* will help us how, my love?
Pariah As all our attempts at disposing of Old King Cole have failed, it is time to call upon the powers of darkness to assist us. This book not only contains magic spells, it also tells of the places where they can be successfully performed.
Peski You mean like ... (*he looks scared and gulps*) ... the Forbidden Forest?
Pariah Yes. That is the nearest one. There are others too which ... Hush! Someone approaches.

Florian enters from DL *with a downcast Debbie*

Florian (*seeing them and bowing*) Your Highnesses.
Pariah Who is that peasant?
Florian Allow me to present Miss Deborah Dumplin.
Peski (*to Debbie, à la Leslie Phillips*) Hello!
Pariah (*snapping at him*) Peski! We do not associate with common riff-raff.
Florian (*angered*) She is *not* common riff-raff! (*He regains his control*) She is our future queen.
Peski
Pariah } (*together, alarmed*) What!!
Florian A short while ago His Majesty chose Debbie ... er ... Miss Dumplin to be his wife.
Pariah Already! (*To Debbie*) But you are not married to him yet?
Debbie (*on the verge of tears*) No ... not yet.

Peski and Pariah show their relief

Florian If you will excuse us, His Majesty is expecting Miss Dumplin at the palace.

He bows to them and leads the tearful Debbie out DR

Act I, Scene 4

Pariah (*urgently*) We have to work fast, Peski. That girl stands between you and the throne. We must get rid of your brother before he has a chance to marry her. Our only hope now lies in the power of magic.
Peski Yes! What does the book say about ... (*he gulps*) ... the Forbidden Forest?
Pariah (*after leafing through the book*) Ah! Here it is! (*Reading*) *The Forbidden Forest!*

There is a flash of lightning and a great clap of thunder

Peski (*scared*) H-how did you do that?
Pariah Listen! (*Reading*) Within the depths of the Forbidden Forest there is a cave containing a pool of great magical power. A person wishing to reverse the progress of time and become younger must immerse themselves in the waters of the pool. The following spell is then cast and the person will emerge from the waters miraculously reduced in age. (*She looks up, her eyes gleaming with devilish cunning*) That's it! That's what we will do to Old King Cole! (*She snaps the book shut and gives a laugh of evil triumph*) Ha! Ha! Ha!
Peski I don't wish to spoil your fun, my little rose thorn, but how is that going to help? We don't want to make my brother *younger*. We want to get rid of him completely.
Pariah And we will! Trust your little Pariah. I know what I'm doing.
Peski But——
Pariah (*looking to off* L) Shh! Your brother is approaching! Leave everything to me. *I* will do the talking.
Peski That'll make a nice change.

Old King Cole enters from DL. *Even the sight of the sinister pair doesn't dispel his happy mood*

King Cole Oh! Hello, you two! Have you heard my wonderful news? I've found a wife!
Pariah (*very smarmy*) Yes, Your Majesty. We have also had the good fortune to meet the young lady concerned.
King Cole You have? Awfully nice little thing, isn't she, what?
Pariah Very charming. May we offer you our congratulations.
King Cole Thank you. Now, I must be getting back to the palace. I expect she'll be there waiting for me by now. (*He crosses to exit* DR)
Pariah (*to Peski, but loud enough for the King to hear*) It's such a shame.
Peski (*genuinely puzzled*) What is?
King Cole (*coming back*) Yes. What's such a shame?
Pariah Well, I ... Oh, it's not my place to say, Your Majesty.

King Cole That's never stopped you before. Come on! Out with it. Has it got something to do with my bride-to-be?
Pariah (*pretending reluctance*) Well ... yes. It's the great difference in your ages ...
King Cole Oh, that! Well, you know the old saying. There's many a good tune played on an old fiddle! I'm sure we'll be very happy together.
Pariah I'm sure you will, Your Majesty. But for how long? It's such a shame that your happiness will be so short-lived. You being so much *older* than her.
King Cole (*pondering*) Mm! I see what you mean. (*Brightening*) Well, it can't be helped. I'll certainly make the most of what years I've got left. We can't turn the clock back, can we?
Pariah That's not true, Your Majesty.
King Cole Eh? What d'you mean?
Pariah There is a way of turning the clock back.
King Cole I'm not taking pills!
Pariah This has nothing to do with pills, Your Majesty. I know of a certain magic pool in which it is possible to shed the years and regain your youth.
King Cole (*to Peski*) Has she been on the Special Brew? (*To Pariah*) You're talking a lot of nonsense. Magic pools indeed! And where *is* this so-called magic pool?
Pariah In — *the Forbidden Forest!*

There is a flash of lightning and a great clap of thunder

Peski (*to King*) I don't know how she does that!
Pariah (*to King, coaxingly*) Imagine. One dip in the pool and you can be young again. As young as your bride-to-be! Just think of all the years you and she can spend — *together.*
King Cole (*wavering*) I ... I don't know ... What would I have to do?
Pariah Just immerse yourself in the waters of the pool. *I* will attend to the rest. All the instructions are in this book.
King Cole And you're sure it will make me younger?
Pariah Positive. I believe Cliff Richard (*or whoever!*) has used it many, many times.
King Cole (*resolved*) Right! Why not! I'll give it a shot! Let's do it at once!
Pariah You won't regret it, Your Majesty. (*Aside to Peski, with an evil cackle*) Hee! Hee! And neither shall we!
Peski (*aside*) I still don't get it, my love.
Pariah (*aside*) You will, Peski, you will.

King Cole Come along, you two! What are we waiting for? Let's get me *rejuvenated!*
Pariah Lead on, Your Majesty! To — *the Forbidden Forest!*

There is a flash of lightning and a great clap thunder

Peski (*to the audience*) I wish I knew how she does that!

King Cole exits DR. *Laughing her evil laugh, Pariah follows him out*

There is another flash of lightning and clap of thunder

Peski jumps with fright and runs out after them

The Lights fade to black-out

Suitably sinister music to cover the scene change, and then the Lights come up on —

Scene 5

The Forbidden Forest

Full set. A very spooky-looking place. The backcloth and side wings represent twisted trees and tangled undergrowth. Mid stage R, *is the entrance to a cave. The shimmering reflection of water is seen coming from inside the cave. Entrances* R *and* L *and at the back*

Weird lighting illuminates the scene and strange noises fill the air. To suitably sinister music, the Chorus and Dancers, as grotesque Creatures, enter from various directions. When they have assembled, they go into their bizarre routine

Song 8

After the number, the Creatures exit in various directions

Pariah sweeps on from L *with the book. She obviously takes great delight in her sinister surroundings*

Pariah Ah! Here we are! *The Forbidden Forest!*

There is a flash of lightning and a clap of thunder

The magic pool must be somewhere in this area, Peski ... (*She realizes she is alone*) Peski? (*Angrily, she calls to off* L) Peski!
Peski (*off* L, *timidly*) Y-Yes?
Pariah Come here!
Peski (*off* L) D-Do I h-have to?
Pariah Yes! Come here at once!

Peski enters very nervously from L. *He looks about him with fear and dread*

What's the matter with you?
Peski It's this forest, my dear. I've never been here before. (*He shivers*) Ugh! It gives me the creeps!
Pariah Nonsense! It's very pleasant. My dear mother often walks here.
Peski (*letting out a terrified yell*) Ahh! (*Looking about in fear*) She's not here now, is she?
Pariah Of course not. (*With sudden alarm*) What have you done with that old fool? You've not lost him, have you?
Peski He's just over there. He had to pop behind a tree.
Pariah I don't wish to know that.
Peski Not for that kind of pop. He wanted to remove his regal robes. He doesn't want to get them wet in the magic pool. And talking of pools, my little poison dart, you still haven't explained how making him younger is going to help us.
Pariah All will be revealed. Trust me.
King Cole (*off* L, *calling*) Hello there! Where are you?
Pariah (*calling back, very sweetly*) Over here, Your Majesty.

King Cole enters from L. *He is now wearing only long red combinations and his crown*

King Cole I say! I hope this won't take long. It's a bit draughty round the royal ramparts.
Pariah No time at all, Your Majesty. We just have to locate the magic pool ... (*She looks towards the cave*) And if I'm not mistaken ... (*Going up to cave and peering inside*) Yes! Here it is! The magic pool!

The King and Peski go up and look into the cave

King Cole By Jove! It looks awfully deep. I'm not very good around water. I get sea-sick standing on the bathmat. (*Getting cold feet*) Look, I ... I've changed my mind. I don't think I'll bother. Best leave well alone. (*He moves away to* L)

Act I, Scene 5   29

Pariah (*going after him*) Wait, Your Majesty! There is nothing to be afraid of. A little wetting is a small sacrifice to pay for regaining your youth. (*Coaxingly*) Think. For just a few seconds under water you can be a young man again. No more rheumatism. No more shortage of breath. No more queuing up to get your pension.
King Cole (*brightening to the idea again*) I'll be able to wear tight jeans again!
Pariah Exactly. And best of all, you will be the same age as your bride-to-be. All those happy years you can spend together.
King Cole Right! Let's do it!

He strides back to the cave, but balks at the entrance. Unceremoniously, Pariah pushes him inside

(*From the cave, with an echo effect*) I say! There's not much room in here!
Pariah (*calling to inside*) Are you in the pool?
King Cole (*from the cave*) No!

There is a yell, followed by a loud splash

I am *now*!

He is heard splashing about and spitting out water

I'm right up to my neck in it! Brr! It's freezing!
Pariah (*calling to the cave*) Stay right where you are, Your Majesty. (*She turns away*) Excellent! (*She gives a fiendish cackle*) Hee! Hee! Hee!
Peski Oh, I get it now. You're hoping he'll die from ... what's the word? Hyper ... Hypermarket.
Pariah Hyperthermia! It's a nice idea, but no. I have a much better plan.
King Cole (*from the cave*) Hurry up, out there! I'm going to end up with frozen assets at this rate!
Pariah (*calling into cave*) It won't be long now, Your Majesty. I just have to cast the magic spell. (*She moves to centre stage and addresses the audience with devilish glee*) The magic spell that will see the end of Old King Cole! (*She gives an evil laugh*) Ha! Ha! Ha! (*She opens the book and searches for the right page*)

As she is doing this, the Creatures emerge from all directions and creep towards the pair

One reaches out and touches Peski on the shoulder. He turns, sees the Creature and gives a "silent" scream. He becomes aware of the others

Peski (*pulling at Pariah's sleeve, terrified*) M-m-my love!
Pariah (*still engrossed in the book*) What is it?
Peski W-We have company! *Look!*

Pariah looks at the Creatures who now surround them. They grunt, wave their arms and make hideous faces. Peski is terrified, but Pariah is completely unmoved

Pariah Oh, yes. I believe they inhabit the forest. On their days off they can be found loitering in [local place]. (*She makes hideous faces at the Creatures*)

With terrified cries, they recoil and retreat into the background

Now to cast the magic spell! (*Reading from the book*)
"O, Powers of darkness and sorcery!
Come to my aid and work for me!"

There is a flash of lightning and a great clap of thunder. Ground mist swirls. Sinister music plays under. With demoniacal laughter, Pariah sweeps up to the cave entrance. She is illuminated by an eerie follow spot

(*Reading from the book*) He who bathes in the magic pool,
        Will soon be made to look a fool!
        Now very old and long in the tooth,
        He wants again the days of his youth.
        But not as a teenager will he be,
        When I have worked my devilry!
        More years I plan to steal away,
        And reduce him to a child at play!
        The powers of darkness I now employ!
        To turn him into — a *ten-year-old boy!*

There is a blinding flash from inside the cave. More thunder and lightning. More laughter from Pariah. Take out follow spot

Ha! Ha! Ha! (*Calling into the cave, very sweetly*) You can come out now — (*contentiously*) Your Majesty!

Little King Cole stumbles out of the cave. King Cole has certainly undergone a terrific transformation. He is now a small ten-year-old boy! He still wears the red combinations (duplicate pair to fit) and his crown has slipped down over his eyes. He is dazed and confused to say the least

Act I, Scene 5   31

(*With triumphant glee*) It worked! Ha! Ha! Ha!

In awe, the King inspects his reduced stature

Little King Cole By Jove! What the ... (*He reacts at the change in his voice*) Oh, dear! (*To Pariah*) I say! Haven't you gone too far? I didn't want to be *this* young! I don't want to have to go to school again!
Pariah Now do you see the brilliance of my plan, Peski? By reducing him to the age of ten he will no longer be a threat to us. To the world Old King Cole has mysteriously disappeared!
Little King Cole But I haven't! I'm right here!
Pariah (*snarling at him*) Be quiet, you little brat! And you won't be needing *this* anymore! (*She snatches the crown from the King's head and gives it to Peski*) For you, my love.
Little King Cole I say! You can't do that! (*Trying to get the crown*) Give me back my crown!
Pariah (*pushing him away*) Get away!
Peski (*slavering over the crown*) At last! Mine! All mine! (*With sudden alarm*) But what will people think when they see me with it?
Pariah We will say we found it lying in the road with no sign of Old King Cole anywhere. It will add realism to his strange and sudden disappearance.
Peski Ah, yes! Very clever, my little hornet's nest.
Little King Cole You pair of villains! You won't get away with this! Just wait till I tell everyone what you've done to me!
Pariah Ha! And who is going to believe a little squirt like you? No one! That's the beauty of my plan.
Peski Yes! (*To the audience*) No one *ever* believes what children say!
Pariah Come, Peski! It is time we told everyone of the amazing and tragic disappearance of Old King Cole!

Laughing their evil laughs, and sneering at the audience, they exit L

The Creatures slowly close in around Little King Cole. Sinister music creeps in

Little King Cole *Wait!* You can't do this to me! *Come back!*

Little King Cole runs to exit L, *but finds the Creatures there. He runs to exit* R, *but finds that way is blocked as well. He backs away, finding himself surrounded by the Creatures. They grunt, wave their arms and make hideous faces at him*

Go away! Don't you know who I am? I am Old King Cole! ... er ... *young* King Cole! Get away from me! Get away! *I command you!*

Gibbering and cackling, the Creatures start to dance around Little King Cole

Reprise of Song 8

The dance starts slowly and then gathers in momentum to become a wild, frenzied affair. Little King Cole is caught up in the middle of it.

Eventually, he manages to break free and escapes by the nearest exit

The Creatures continue their wild contortions, ending in a bizarre tableau, as —

— *the* CURTAIN *falls*

ACT II

Scene 1

The Town Square

As Act I, Scene 3

The Townsfolk are discovered going about their business. The Fiddlers enter. A song and dance follows

Song 9

After the number, Dotty enters from R

Dotty (*greeting the audience*) Hello, folks! Hi, kids! It's lovely to see you all again. (*To someone*) Yes, even *you!* (*To all*) I wonder how my Debbie's getting on at the palace. Oh, I'm so excited for her. And I can't wait for the wedding. It's bound to be a big posh do. (*With sudden alarm*) 'Ere! I hope they're not expectin' *me* to do the cookin'! I am the mother of the bride, after all. All I'm expected to do is weep buckets, not slave over a hot microwave. And another thing —

Little King Cole runs on from L. *He sees Dotty and rushes to her*

Little King Cole Dotty!
Dotty Eh? 'Ere! Don't be so familiar! Who are you? And go and put some clothes on!
Little King Cole Never mind that. You've got to help me!
Dotty I'll do nothing of the sort! Go away, you little ragamuffin! Stop botherin' me! Shoo!
Little King Cole Please! You must listen to me!
1st Male (*coming forward and grabbing the king*) Oy! Didn't you hear the lady?
Dotty What lady? Oh! He means little me!
Little King Cole (*to Man*) How dare you! Take your hands off me! I am your King!

Dotty and the others roar with laughter

1st Male And I'm [current personality]!
Little King Cole I'm telling you the truth!
1st Female He's potty!
2nd Male Cracked!
Dotty Yes! He's obviously suffering from diffusions of glandular.
1st Male (*to the King*) Go on! Get out of here!
Little King Cole But, I ——
1st Male All right! You asked for it!

He picks up the King and carrying him to exit L, *deposits him off stage*

The others laugh

Dotty (*to the audience*) That'll teach [local place] to send their surplus nitwits 'ere!

The Herald enters from R

Look out! Here's Hornblower! (*Or something to suit*)

The Herald blows his trumpet. Fanfare sounds

Florian enters from R, *followed by Debbie*

Florian (*to all*) Your attention, please! I have an important announcement to make. His Majesty, King Cole, has failed to return to the royal palace.

Reaction from the others

Dotty Oh, no! He's run out on our Debbie already! (*To the audience*) You can't trust anyone these days, can yah!
Florian He was last seen here in the town square. I must ask you all to carry out a thorough search. Every street, house, shop, park and public building.
Dotty Even the ones in [place where local public toilets are situated]?
Florian All! The King *must* be found.
Dotty (*to Townsfolk*) Well, don't just stand there! Let's kind of thing ... I mean ... find the king!

Dotty, the Fiddlers and the Townsfolk rush out in various directions

Florian nods at the Herald

The Herald exits R

Act II, Scene 1   35

Debbie (*overjoyed*) Oh, Florian. It seems that good fortune has smiled on us.
Florian How? Our king appears to be missing.
Debbie Exactly. That means you and I can be together.
Florian (*with a sigh*) If only it were that simple.
Debbie What do you mean?
Florian (*taking her in his arms*) Oh, Debbie. I love you with all my heart. But I also love my king. I have a loyalty to him. It is my duty to protect him at all costs. Even to the extent of my own happiness.
Debbie (*to the audience*) I love him dearly, but he's such a workaholic!

There is a commotion off R. *This causes the lovers to part*

The Herald enters from R

Florian What is it? Has the King been found?
Herald Nah. It's some little kid. Insists on talkin' to you. 'E's two sandwiches short of a picnic, if you arst me.
Florian Why do you say that?
Herald 'E reckons 'e's King Cole!
Florian I see. Bring him here.
Herald Don't say I didn't warn yah. (*He calls to off* R) Come 'ere, you!

Little King Cole enters from R

Little King Cole (*rushing to Florian*) Look what they did to me! You've got to do something! You've got to help me!
Florian Just a minute. Who *are* you?
Little King Cole I'm the King! King Cole!
Herald See wot I mean? 'E's nuts!
Little King Cole (*to him*) How dare you! I will have you demoted to triangle player for that!
Florian All right, young man. You've had your fun. Why don't you run along home now.
Little King Cole But, I tell you ——
Florian (*to the Herald*) See him on his way.
Herald Wiv pleasure! Come on, you!

The Herald frogmarches the protesting King out R

There is a commotion off L. *Pariah and Peski rush on from* L. *They are followed by some of the Townsfolk. At the same time, Dotty, the Fiddlers, and the rest of the Townsfolk enter from* R

Pariah Listen, all of you! We have grave news to impart. Old King Cole has disappeared!
Dotty No, he ain't! He's just gone missing. He's probably hidin' in the [local pub/club].
Pariah He has *not* just gone missing! He has disappeared completely!
Peski It's true. All we found was *this!* (*He produces the crown from under his cloak and holds it up*)

Reaction from the others

Florian The King's crown!
Pariah It was lying in the roadway near — *the Forbidden Forest!*

There is a flash of lightning and a great clap of thunder. All react

Dotty (*to the audience*) Typical! I've just 'ung me undies out!
Pariah We searched everywhere but found no sign of the King. (*Darkly*) It is my belief he has been spirited away by the supernatural forces that inhabit the forest. I fear he is lost to us forever!
Florian You can't be serious.
Dotty I dunno. She could be right. I lost summit meself in that forest years ago.
Florian What?
Dotty Er ... never you mind. It's a very spooky place, that's all I know. Strange and dialogical things can happen there.

The Townsfolk agree with this

Florian The King may have simply wandered into the forest and got himself lost. Come, we will go there at once and find him.

The Townsfolk back away, shaking their heads and mumbling

Florian What's the matter with you?
1st Male (*scared*) You won't catch me going into that forest!
1st Female Nor me!
Others Nor me! Nor me!
Florian This is superstitious nonsense!
Pariah It is not! The dark powers of the forest are well known. We have to face the truth. (*With O.T.T. sadness*) Our beloved King Cole has been taken from us!
Townsfolk (*agreeing, very sadly*) She's right! Yes! Shame! Dear, dear! (*Etc.*)

Act II, Scene 1   37

Pariah But cheer up! We have a new king to take his place. Put it on, Peski!
Peski Oh, Yes! (*He puts the crown on his head and struts about*)
Pariah (*to all*) Behold! Your new king! King Peski!

Shock and consternation from all the others

(*Snarling at the Townsfolk*) Don't just stand there, you putrid peasants! Show respect to your new king! (*Preening herself*) And his queen!

The dismayed Townsfolk bow and curtsy to them

Dotty (*to Florian*) We can't let those two nasties take over. You're a diploprat, do something about it!
Florian I intend to. (*Marching across to the bowing Townsfolk*) Stop that at once! (*To Peski*) This is completely out of order. You can't just make yourself king.
Dotty 'Ear! 'Ear!
Pariah And why not? The old king has gone. As his brother, my husband is next in line to the throne.
Peski And I've got *this*! (*He points to the crown*) So — (*he blows a raspberry*) to you!
Florian I am still not convinced that King Cole *has* gone. I intend going to the forest in search of him.
Pariah Pah! Do as you like, but you won't find him. And don't bother coming back. You're sacked!
Florian (*indignantly*) You're too late! *I resign!*

Florian marches out R. *Debbie runs out after him*

Peski
Pariah } (*together*) Good riddance! (*Laughing evilly*) Ha! Ha! Ha!
Pariah And while we're on the subject. (*To Fiddlers*) You three fools are sacked as well.
Fiddlers Eh?
Pariah There's no need for that "Old King Cole is a merry old soul" rubbish anymore.
Peski And your dopey songs and dances have become a bore! So —
Pariah You *are* the weakest link!
Both Goodbye!

With bowed heads, the Fiddlers file out R

Peski
Pariah } (*together, with more evil laughter*) Ha! Ha! Ha!

Dotty (*to the audience*) Oh! The rotten ... so-and-sos! (*She reacts as she sees the evil pair moving in her direction. To them, with a sickly grin*) Hello. Can I help you?
Pariah You've never liked us, have you?
Dotty Compared to who? Freddie Krueger?
Peski Well, we don't like *you* either! And your cooking is rubbish!
Dotty (*indignantly*) Oh! That hurts!
Pariah It certainly does! It always gives me chronic heartburn.
Dotty Really? I didn't know you had one.
Peski We'll be eating at [local upmarket restaurant] from now on.
Dotty And I hope you get indigestion and can't find the Gaviscon!
Pariah So we won't be needing you anymore. You're ——
Peski Please let *me* say it, my love. (*Pointing his finger at Dotty*) You're fired!
Dotty Good! I don't wanna cook for you anyway! I'd rather work at [local school]. You're a pair of horrible, ugly, naughty nasties! (*To the audience*) Aren't they, folks?
Audience Yes!
Pariah (*to the audience*) And so are you!
Peski (*to the audience*) Oh, yes, you are!
Audience Oh, no, we're not!

This continues ad-lib

Dotty You tell 'em, folks!
Pariah (*snarling at Dotty*) Any more from you and we'll not just *sack* you, we'll *rack* you!
Dotty (*yelling*) TAXI!!

Dotty beats a very hasty exit R

Peski
Pariah } (*together, even more evil laughter*) Ha! Ha! Ha!
Peski (*exalted*) Oh! The power! (*To the audience*) I told you I'd be king, didn't I? Well, now that I am, I intend to make you all *squirm* and *grovel!*
Pariah Let's have a practice on this riff-raff!
Peski (*to Townsfolk*) Yes! Let's see you all grovelling!
Pariah On your knees before your king, you rabble!
Peski Grovel! Grovel!

The Townsfolk get to their knees and bow their heads

(*Elated*) Oh! This is what I've always dreamed of! Ultimate power! And I owe it all to you, my little poison ivy!
Pariah Do you know what I feel like doing, Peski?
Peski (*hopefully*) Yes, my love?
Pariah I feel like singing!
Peski (*disappointed*) Oh!
Pariah Yes! A song to celebrate. (*To Townsfolk*) And you can join in — or else!

Song 10

A comically "evil" song and dance for Pariah and Peski. Under threat, the Townsfolk are forced to join in. It ends with Peski and Pariah posing in arrogant fashion with the Townsfolk grovelling before them. The Lights fade to black-out

Music to cover the scene change, and then the Lights come up on —

Scene 2

Outside the Palace Gates

As Act I, Scene 2

Florian strides on from DR, *heading for exit* DL

Debbie runs on from DR

Debbie (*calling to him*) Florian! ... Wait!
Florian (*stopping and going to her*) What is it? I have to get to the forest and find the King.
Debbie But why bother? You heard what they said. He's gone.
Florian Surely you don't believe that rubbish about him being spirited away.
Debbie Well, there have always been strange stories connected with that forest.
Florian Exactly. Stories, that's all they are. No, I'm convinced the King is still there and I'm going to find him.
Debbie And if you do, what will happen to us? He'll marry me and we'll be parted forever. Is that what you want?
Florian Of course not. But as I explained before, I have a duty to my king. I'm sorry, Debbie.

Debbie Then let me go with you.
Florian If you wish. (*With mild sarcasm*) Won't you be frightened in the forest?
Debbie Not as long as I'm with you.
Florian Come, then. I hope we find him before nightfall.
Debbie (*aside to the Audience*) And I hope we don't!

They are about to exit DL, *when Little King Cole enters there*

Little King Cole I must speak to you!
Florian Oh, not you again! Out of my way, boy! I have to find the King!
Little King Cole But I *am* the King!

Florian pushes Little King Cole aside and exits with Debbie DL

(*Despairingly*) Oh! Will no one listen to me?!

A very downcast Dotty enters from DR. *She is followed by the equally miserable Fiddlers*

Little King Cole Dotty!
Dotty Oh, not *you* again! Go away!
Little King Cole Please ——
Dotty I'm not in the mood for your nonsense. I'm too upset. (*Pouting*) I've just been given the sack!
Fiddlers And us!
Little King Cole What! *Who* gave you the sack?
Dotty Who d'you think? The gruesome twosome! Peski and Pariah!
Little King Cole They had no right to do that! Why?
Dotty My face doesn't fit.
Little King Cole That's true, but they still had no right.
Dotty Well, they ... why I am I discussin' this with you? Go away!
Little King Cole You must listen to me! I've been ...
Dotty (*to the Fiddlers*) D'ya mind? (*She jerks her thumb to exit* DL)

The Fiddlers pick up the King, and carry him to exit DL

Little King Cole (*wailing, as goes*) Oh, no! Not again!

The Fiddlers deposit him off stage, and then return

Dotty (*to the audience, tearfully*) Oooh! I don't know what I'm gonna do now, folks. I've lost my job! I've lost my chance of being a royal! I've lost everything! (*Wailing*) Waaaagh!!

Act II, Scene 2   41

The Fiddlers move over and comfort her

Fiddlers Cheer up.
Dotty (*sniffing*) Thanks. You're a great comfort to me.
Fiddlers Our pleasure.
Dotty 'Ere! There's something I've always wanted to ask. Do you three do everything together?
Fiddlers Yes.
Dotty What, *everything?*
Fiddlers Yes.
Dotty Crikey! It must get crowded in there! Oh, I'm so depressed, I'm thinking of emigratin' to [local place]! I must get another job soon, or I won't be able to pay for my [topical reference]! Now, what can ... Hey! I've got an idea. As we've all been sacked, why don't the four of us form a group? I'm a very good singist, y'know. (*She does a loud, tuneless singing of scales*) Oh, yes! I'd have got on [TV reality show] if it hadn't been for the restraining order. Go on! What d'you say?

The Fiddlers go into a huddle

(*To the audience*) I bet they're discussin' my enormous attributes.

The Fiddlers come out of the huddle and nod to Dotty

Does that mean we can form a group?
Fiddlers Yes.
Dotty Great! Now, what shall we try? I know! How about something like *this!*

Song 11

This is a comical send-up of a noisy rock number. It should be played over the sound system. Flashing lights and smoke, etc. Dotty and the Fiddlers mime to the words and gyrate about. It ends in a crescendo of noise, lights and flashes

Dotty (*to the audience, on her knees and exhausted*) Lady Gaga, eat yer heart out! (*To Fiddlers*) What do you think? Want to try it again?
Fiddlers (*exhausted*) No!
Dotty (*staggering to her feet, gasping*) No stamina ... that's your trouble.

Little King Cole enters from DL

Little King Cole (*rushing to her*) Dotty!
Dotty (*groaning*) Oh, no! Not you *again!* Go away! Why aren't you in school? It can't be another flippin' 'oliday!
Little King Cole (*grabbing her by the arms and shaking her*) You *will* listen to me! *You will!*
Dotty Oy! Oy! Ger off! You're too young to manhandle me! (*She pushes him away*) Come back when you're older!
Little King Cole Dotty, please! I *am* King Cole! You must believe me!
Dotty Oh, change the record. Why don't you try bein' [topical/local reference] instead? (*She makes for exit* DR)
Little King Cole (*pursuing her*) It was Pariah! She did this to me!
Dotty Did what?
Little King Cole Turned me into what you see. A ten-year-old boy!
Dotty (*to Fiddlers*) You keep him talking while I call an ambulance.
Little King Cole It's true. (*Indicating the audience*) *They* know it's true. (*To them*) Don't you?
Audience Yes!
Dotty Oh, no, it isn't!
Audience Oh, yes, it is!

This continues ad-lib

Dotty (*to the King*) Well, I still don't believe it!
Little King Cole Pariah did it so that Peski could be king. I went into the magic pool as Old King Cole and came out as Bart Simpson.
Dotty You've got an very vivid imagination, I'll say that for yah. Have you thought of writing for the [local newspaper]?
Little King Cole (*struck by an idea*) I know! Why didn't I think of it before? I can *prove* I am Old King Cole.
Dotty (*jeeringly*) Oh, yeah! How?
Little King Cole By telling you something that only *he* could know about. (*He whispers something in Dotty's ear*)

Dotty reacts

Dotty Oh! Was that when I ...?

The King nods

And you ...?

The King nods

Act II, Scene 3   43

And then we both ...?

The King nods

(*Dismayed*) Crikey! You really are Old King Cole! Oh, Your Maj! How can you ever forgive me?
Little King Cole Never mind that now. I've got to get back to normal before that dastardly brother of mine makes himself king.
Dotty You're too late, Your Imperial Leather, he already has! There's only one thing to do. You'll have to take another bath in that magic pool and grow up — *fast*.
Little King Cole You're right, but there's a problem. To make it work a magic spell has to be cast. That spell is in a book which Pariah holds.
Dotty Then you'll have to get it from her.
Little King Cole You mean steal it?
Dotty (*à la Churchill, the dog*) Oh, yes!
Little King Cole How? They'll never let me into the palace.
Dotty Leave that to me, Your Little Maj! (*To Fiddlers*) Come on, you three! We'll need your help.

They all exit DR

The Lights fade to black-out

Music to cover the scene change, and then the Lights come up on —

SCENE 3

The Royal Palace

As Act I, Scene 1

Peski is seated on the throne. Pariah stands at his side. Both are now wearing regal robes and Pariah has a crown. The Herald is standing at the back, looking bored. The Pages are performing a dance while the Courtiers are grouped at the sides, singing

Song 12

After the number, with some trepidation, they all face the throne and bow

Pariah What a pathetic display! I've seen better dancing at the zoo! And as for that so-called singing! Ugh! Deplorable!

Peski I quite agree, my love. I thought the [local choral/operatic society] were pretty awful until I heard them! (*To Courtiers*) You lot had better pull your socks up, or you'll be out on your ear.
Pariah And not your musical ear either, because you haven't got one!

Both roar with laughter at this "joke"

Now, go away, all of you! You're making the place look untidy.

The chastened Courtiers and Pages shuffle out in various directions

The Herald remains

(*To the Herald*) Didn't you hear?
Herald Wot?
Peski Clear off!
Herald An' you!
Pariah What?!
Herald Achoo! ... I sneezed.

Behind their backs the Herald pokes out his tongue, and then exits at the back

Peski (*wriggling about with delight*) Mmm! This throne is soooo comfortable!
Pariah And it suits you so well, my love. Tell me, now that you are the King have you given any thought as to what we should do about — them! (*She points to the audience*)
Peski (*standing up*) Ah! Yes!

They move forward, sneering at the audience

They've been very rude to us, haven't they?
Pariah Very. I think they should be made to suffer some unspeakable punishment.
Peski So do I. What do you suggest, my little bindweed?

The Herald enters from L

(*Snapping at him*) What do you want?
Herald There's someone 'ere to see yah.
Peski Who is it?
Herald (*with great pleasure*) Lady Dragonia! Yer mother-in-law!

Act II, Scene 3　　　　　　　　　　　　　　　　　　　　　　　　45

Peski (*shrinking with fear and loathing*) Oh, no!
Pariah (*to Herald*) My mamma! Show her in at once.

Lady Dragonia sweeps on from L. *She is a formidable elderly lady with bizarre dress sense*

Dragonia There is no need! I am in already!
Peski (*cringing*) Yaaah!
Dragonia (*bearing down on Peski*) So! Is it true that you are now the King?
Peski (*meekly*) Yes, Mother-in-law.
Dragonia I am very pleased to hear it.
Peski Thank you, Mother-in-law.
Dragonia Because you are no good for anything else!
Herald Nice one!

Chortling to himself, the Herald exits L

Pariah It's lovely to see you, Mamma. Isn't it, Peski?
Peski Lovely. I never hoped to see your mother —
Dragonia (*sharply*) What?!
Peski (*hastily*) Looking so well.
Dragonia I can only stay for a short while.
Peski (*sotto voce*) Good.
Dragonia Just a week or two.
Peski (*groaning*) Oooh!
Dragonia I have really called to consult the book of magic spells I lent to you. Be so good as to bring it to me.
Pariah Yes, Mamma.

Pariah exits R

A deathly silence falls. Dragonia slowly circles Peski, looking him up and down. He remains facing front, cringing and expecting the worst. Eventually, her voice makes him jump

Dragonia So! Do you like being a king?
Peski Yes, Mother-in-law.
Dragonia Do you enjoy having power over people?
Peski Yes, Mother-in-law.
Dragonia (*glaring at him*) So do *I*! And don't you forget it.
Peski Yes, Mother-in-law ...! I mean ... No, Mother-in-law.

Pariah enters from R with the book

Dragonia (*taking the book*) Ah! My precious book of magic spells! I have a troublesome neighbour to whom I wish to do something *very* unpleasant. She keeps complaining about my barbecue. She says that my cooking of eye of newt and wing of bat is affecting her roses. Tiresome woman! I want to teach her a lesson she will not forget. Now, let me see. What unspeakable thing can I do to her? (*She turns the pages and reads*) Boils? ... Warts? ... Facial hair? ... Bandy legs? ... No, she already has all those! I must delve deeper.

Still consulting the book, Dragonia exits R

Pariah (*turning on Peski*) I do wish you would show Mamma a little more courtesy.
Peski (*aside*) I'd like to show her the door!
Pariah What was that?

But Peski is saved by the entrance of the Herald from L

What is it now?
Herald Someone else to see yah.
Peski Who is it this time?
Herald Dotty Dumplin.
Peski We sacked her. What does she want?
Herald Says she's 'ere to hapologize.
Pariah Ha! Hoping to get her job back no doubt.
Peski Send her away.
Pariah Wait, my love. (*With evil relish*) It would be nice to see her *grovelling* and *begging!*
Peski (*with equal delight*) It would indeed, my little stinging nettle! (*To Herald*) Send her right in.

The Herald exits L

Anticipating the pleasure to come, Peski resumes his seat on the throne. Pariah takes up her position at his side

The Herald enters from L

Herald (*announcing*) Mrs Dotty Dumplin! 'Ere to grovel!

A very penitent Dotty enters from L. She walks slowly towards the throne with her head bowed

Act II, Scene 3   47

The curious Courtiers enter from R and L and at the back

The Herald exits L

Peski What do you want?
Dotty (*meekly*) I was very rude to you and I've come to say I'm sorry.
Pariah Do it properly then! Down on your knees!
Dotty Eh?!
Peski Yes! Grovel before me!

With great difficulty, Dotty gets down on her knees. Peski and Pariah enjoy the spectacle

Peski
Pariah } (*together*) *Lower!*

Dotty manages to put her forehead on the ground

Peski
Pariah } (*together*) *Lower!*

Comic business as Dotty tries to comply. She topples forward and sprawls flat out. Peski and Pariah laugh

Dotty (*turning her head to the front*) That's yer lot! Any lower and I'd be in Australia!
Pariah Now, repeat this. I am very sorry.
Dotty I am very sorry.
Pariah Because.
Dotty Because.
Pariah I am an ugly old trout!
Dotty You are an ugly old trout!

Peski laughs at this. Pariah gives him a fierce glare and his laughter is cut short

Pariah (*to Dotty*) Get up!
Dotty (*to the audience*) Is there a fork lift in the house? (*She struggles to her feet*)
Pariah I suppose you'd like your job back.
Dotty Yes, please.
Pariah (*with evil relish*) Well, you can't have it!

Peski *Get out!*

Peski and Pariah cackle together

Dotty But I said I'm sorry. I've even brought you a present.
Peski What sort of present?
Dotty (*calling to off* L) Bring it in!

The Fiddlers enter from L. *They are pushing a trolley on which is mounted a huge cake. See Production Notes*

(*Proudly*) There! What d'you think of that!
Peski (*rising*) Is it a cake?
Dotty No, it's a new conservatory (*or something topical*)! Of course it's a cake. And it's all for you. To say how sorry I am. It's a sort of humble pie cake.
Pariah (*suspiciously*) It didn't take you long to bake it.
Dotty Well ... it's one I prepared earlier.

A few of the Courtiers have come forward to inspect the cake

(*To them*) Oy! Stop droolin' on it! That's for our lovely royals! Go on! Beat it! All of you!

Dotty and the Fiddlers shoo the Courtiers out

The Courtiers exit in various directions

As soon as they have gone, Dotty gets down to the real business in hand

Right! (*To Fiddlers*) Grab 'em!

Two Fiddlers grab the startled Peski and Pariah and hold them firmly. Dotty and the other Fiddler remove the top of the cake. Little King Cole pops up from inside

Peski
Pariah } (*together, aghast*) *You!!*
Little King Cole Yes! It is I! Old ... er ... Young King Cole!

Dotty helps him to the ground

The Fiddler pushes the trolley off stage L, *and then returns*

Act II, Scene 3   49

Little King Cole (*confronting Peski and Pariah*) As soon as I'm back to normal you two tricksters will be made to pay dearly for this. I want that book!
Pariah What book?
Dotty Well, he doesn't mean the latest Argos catalogue! The book of tragic smells ... er ... magic spells! Hand it over!
Pariah Never!
Dotty Hand it over, or I'll forget I'm a lady and belt the pair of yah! (*Raising her fist*) Startin' with pesky Peski!
Peski (*terrified*) Lady Dragonia's got it!
Dotty Who?
Peski Pariah's mother!
Pariah (*glaring at him*) Peski!
Dotty (*incredulously*) She's got a mother?! Crikey! I always thought she came as a flat pack from Ikea!
Little King Cole Where is she?
Peski (*indicating off* R) In there!

Dotty and the King rush out R

Pariah You fool, Peski!
Peski I had to tell them, my love. I'm allergic to blood! Especially my own!

Dotty and the King rush back in

Little King Cole There's no one there! Where is she?

The captives are genuinely puzzled

The Herald enters from L

Dotty (*to Herald*) Hey, you! We're lookin' for Lady Dragon's den, or whatever 'er name is. Have you seen her?
Herald Yeah. She just left the palace.
Little King Cole Where did she go?
Herald 'Ow should I know? I'm not 'er kipper! (*He turns to go*)
Pariah Wait! Can't you see we're in trouble here? I command you to help us!
Herald I'm on a break! (*He goes*)
Dotty (*to Pariah*) Where's yer momma gone? (*Singing it*) "Where's yer momma gone?"
Pariah I don't know!
Dotty (*to Peski*) Do you?

Peski (*cringing*) No!
Little King Cole We're wasting precious time. Let's go and find the woman and get that book.
Dotty You're right! Come on! (*To Fiddlers*) Don't take your eyes off those two!
Fiddlers Right!

Dotty and the King run out R

The Fiddlers release Peski and Pariah but continue to stare hard at them

Peski (*aside to Pariah*) What are we going to do?
Pariah (*aside*) Leave it to me. (*To Fiddlers*) It is him, isn't it?
Fiddlers Who?
Pariah Johnny Depp. (*Or other current media personality*)
Fiddlers Where?
Pariah (*pointing to* L) Over there!

The Fiddlers rush to look off L

Pariah and Peski quickly make their escape R

The Fiddlers turn and realize they have been tricked

Fiddlers Oh, no! (*To the audience*) Which way did they go?
Audience That way!
Fiddlers (*pointing to back*) This way?
Audience No! *That* way!
Fiddlers Oh, *this* way! Thanks!

Bumping into each other, the Fiddlers rush to exit R

The Lights fade to black-out

Music to cover the scene change, and then the lights come up on —

Scene 4

Outside the Palace Gates

As Act I, Scene 2

Act II, Scene 4   51

Still consulting the book, Lady Dragonia enters DR. *She pauses at* C, *having found what she is looking for*

Dragonia Ah! Here it is! I've found it! The perfect spell to cast on that troublesome neighbour of mine. (*Reading*) Spell for uncontrollable flatulence. This spell is guaranteed to cause your victim total humiliation and complete embarrassment. (*Looking up, with glee*) Perfect! Just the thing! Especially when she's having one of her dinner parties, or making a speech at the [local] WI. That will take the wind out of her sails, or — *put it in!* (*She laughs*) Ha! Ha! Now, I must find a suitable venue in which to cast the spell. Somewhere that has the right kind of demonic atmosphere. Ah, yes! I know the very place. *The Forbidden Forest!*

There is a flash of lightning and a great clap of thunder

(*To off stage*) When I need your assistance, I will ask for it!

Dragonia makes for exit DL

At the same time, Dotty and Little King Cole enter DR

Dotty Oy! Just a minute!

Dragonia stops and turns

Have you seen an old woman with a —
Little King Cole Look! That's the book! It's her! (*To Dragonia*) Give me that book!
Dragonia What is the meaning of this? How dare you accost me in the street. Do you know who I am?
Dotty Yeah! You're Nightmare Nellie's mum. I can see the family resonance! Now, hand over that book!
Dragonia (*clutching the book*) I most certainly will not!
Dotty Don't make me have to throw my weight about.
Dragonia Huh! You would need a crane to do that!
Dotty I'm warnin' you! I can turn very ugly.
Dragonia Really? I thought you already had!
Dotty That's it! You asked for it! (*She stamps on Dragonia's toe*)

With a yell, Dragonia drops the book and hops about in agony. Dotty quickly grabs the book and holds it up in triumph

(*To the audience*) That'll teach 'er to mess with a former pupil of [local school]! Come on, Little Maj! Let's get you back to normal!

Dotty and Little King Cole run out DL

Dragonia continues to hop about on one leg

Peski and Pariah enter from DR

Pariah Mamma!
Peski Why is she dancing?
Dragonia (*limping over to him*) Why are *you* such an idiot?! I am *not* dancing, you imbecile! I have just been assaulted! A very peculiar woman and a small boy attacked me. I happen to be in a great deal of pain!
Peski I'm glad.
Dragonia *What?!*
Peski How sad.
Pariah (*urgently*) And the book of magic spells? Did they take it?
Dragonia Take *it!* They *stole* it from me! What on earth could that woman and a little brat want with my precious book?
Pariah They want to change him back.
Dragonia Change *who* back?
Pariah The little brat. He's King Cole.
Dragonia King Cole! Have you taken leave of your senses, Pariah? King Cole is an *old man*! Really! Being married to this nincompoop has turned your brain.
Peski (*protesting*) Oh! I say!
Dragonia (*rounding on him*) *You* will say *nothing!*
Pariah It is true, Mamma. I contrived to make King Cole enter the magic pool in the forest. Using your book of spells, I changed him into a ten-year-old boy!
Dragonia Whatever for?
Pariah So that Peski could take over the throne. Everyone believes that Old King Cole has disappeared.
Dragonia I see. That explains it. (*To Peski*) I didn't think you had been made king by popular demand.
Peski Isn't she clever? (*He snuggles up to Pariah*) My little Venus flytrap!
Dragonia Stop that at once! It's revolting. (*Gravely*) Well, I must say, I think you have played a very dirty trick on Old King Cole. (*Then with a sly grin*) But an ingenious one! Congratulations, Pariah! (*She gives Pariah a peck on the cheek*)
Pariah Thank you, Mamma.
Dragonia And congratulations to you, Peski.

He cringes, anticipating a kiss, but thankfully doesn't get one

Act II, Scene 4   53

You have obviously married a chip off the old block. So, this woman intends to change the King back, does she?
Peski
Pariah } (*together*) Yes.
Dragonia Then why are we standing here talking?! Let us go to the forest and stop her!

They all move to the exit DL. *Peski gets there first and Dragonia pulls him back*

Where are your manners?

She waves him aside and sweeps out, followed by Pariah

Peski (*to the audience*) I *must* remain king! Even if it's only to have that old boot banished!
Dragonia (*off, bellowing*) Peski!
Peski Or beheaded! (*Calling, sweetly*) Coming, Mother-in-law!

Peski exits DL

The Fiddlers rush on from DR

Fiddlers (*to the audience*) Have you seen them?
Audience Yes!
Fiddlers Which way did they go?
Audience That way!
Fiddlers (*pointing into the auditorium*) This way? Right!

Despite the cries of protest, they come down into the auditorium. Comic business as they search among the audience

They're not here!
Audience That way!
Fiddlers Where?
Audience That way! Out there! (*Etc.*)
Fiddlers Oh, *that* way!

The Fiddlers go back on to the stage and rush out DL

As they exit, the Lights fade to black-out. Music to cover the scene change, and then the Lights come up on —

Scene 5

The Forbidden Forest

As Act I, Scene 5

A flash of lightning and a clap of thunder opens the scene. As it is now night time, the place looks even more spooky and sinister. Ground mist swirls

The Creatures emerge from various directions. They go into a short reprise of their number

Reprise of Song 8

After the number, Debbie is heard calling off R

Debbie (*off* R, *calling*) Florian! ... Where are you? ... Florian?!

The Creatures scuttle away and hide in the background

Debbie enters from R. *She is frightened and looks nervously about her*

(*Calling*) Florian?! ... Oh, where *is* he? ... (*Calling again*) Florian?... Oh, dear! (*To the audience*) I wish we hadn't split up to search for King Cole. I'm completely lost! I've never been in this forest before. It's so ... so dark and creepy! Goodness knows what horrible things are lurking here, waiting to ... (*Calling, desperately*) Florian! ... Where are you?!

Unseen by her, the Creatures emerge from hiding. A couple of them creep up behind Debbie. The audience shout out warnings

(*To the audience*) What's the matter?
Audience Behind you!
Debbie Behind me? Is it Florian playing tricks? I bet it is. Well, I'll soon ——

Debbie turns and is confronted by the Creatures. She screams and runs away, only to find herself surrounded by the other Creatures. They close in on her. She screams

Help!! ... Florian!!... Help me!!

Act II, Scene 5   55

Florian rushes on from L. *He strides threateningly towards the Creatures*

Florian Leave her alone! ... Get away from her! ... *Get away!*

The Creatures scatter and run out in various directions

Debbie rushes into Florian's arms

Debbie Oh, Florian!
Florian (*comforting her*) It's all right. You're safe.
Debbie Those awful creatures! What *are* they?
Florian I'm not sure. They've gone now.

A slight pause while they embrace

Debbie I take it you had no luck finding Old King Cole.
Florian No. (*With a smile*) And I suppose you're hoping I never will.
Debbie I know it's selfish of me, Florian, but I can't help it. All I can think about is *us* and our happiness.
Florian I have a feeling that everything is going to turn out right. You know the old saying — true love will find a way.

Song 13

Romantic duet. The lighting takes on a romantic feel. After the number, it reverts to the previous sinister setting

Debbie Do you really think that everything is going to be all right, Florian?
Florian Yes, I do. But in the meantime, we still have to find the King. (*Taking her hand*) Come on.

They exit L

Little King Cole enters from R

Little King Cole (*looking about him*) This place looks familiar, Dotty. I'm sure it's near here ... (*He finds he is alone*) Dotty?

Dotty creeps on backwards from R. *She is clutching the book and is very scared*

Dotty Ooo! This place gives me the willies! It's worse than the [local pub/club] car park at chuckin' out time! (*Calling, timidly*) Your Maj? ... W-Where are you?
Little King Cole (*right behind her*) Here!
Dotty (*yelling with fright*) Ahhgh! Oh, don't *do* that! Me whole life flashed before me! All twenty-five years of it!
Little King Cole I recognize this spot.
Dotty Well, don't pick it or it'll never get better.
Little King Cole (*exploring upstage*) The magic pool ... it was somewhere ... (*Finding the cave entrance*) Ah! Here it is!
Dotty (*scuttling up to him*) Where?
Little King Cole Inside that cave.
Dotty (*peering in*) Oh, yeah! Huh! A bit primitive, innit? They need to get Bob the Builder in! (*Or TV interior designer*)

Dotty continues to peer inside

Two of the bigger Creatures creep on from L. *One clamps his paw over Little King Cole's mouth. The pair of them carry or drag him out* L

(*Still looking in cave*) Well, in you go, Yer Maj. The sooner we get this over with the better. (*She turns*) Maj? (*Looking about*) Little Maj? Where are yah? (*To the audience*) Where did 'e go, kids?
Audience They took him! (*Etc.*)
Dotty Who took him? Was it someone nice?
Audience No!
Dotty Who was it then?
Audience The monsters/creatures!
Dotty (*scared*) D-Did you s-s-say monsters/creatures?
Audience Yes!
Dotty Oh, no! I might have known! Ooh! D'you think I should go and look for him?
Audience Yes!
Dotty Or shall I go home? Yes, I think I'll go home!

She quickly heads for exit R

Audience *No!*
Dotty (*coming back*) What! You really want me, a poor defenceless woman, to go lookin' for him?
Audience Yes!
Dotty I know you lot! You just want something nasty to happen to me, don't yah? (*To someone*) Especially *you!* All right! I'll do it! They

Act II, Scene 5   57

don't call me the [superhero] of [local place] for nothing! Which way did they go?
Audience *That way!*
Dotty (*pointing to* R) This way?
Audience *No! The other way!*
Dotty This way? Right! (*She strides to exit* L, *and then falters*) Are you sure they were monsters/creatures?
Audience *Yes!*
Dotty Are they big ones? Or little tiny weenie ones?
Audience *Big ones!*
Dotty Just my luck! (*She gulps*) Well, if you don't see me again it's been nice knowin' you! (*She turns to exit*) Oooh! Where's Doctor Who when you need 'im!

With fear and trepidation, she creeps out L

Florian and Debbie enter from up R, *crossing to exit up* L

Florian (*calling, as they cross*) Your Majesty! ... Where are you? ... Your Majesty!

They exit up L

Little King Cole runs on from DL, *being pursued by the two Creatures. They chase him around the stage, and then out up* R

Dragonia enters from DR, *followed by Pariah and Peski. They make straight for the cave and peer inside*

Pariah They aren't here. We've beaten them to it.
Peski Perhaps they've already been and changed him back!
Dragonia I doubt it. If they had, King Cole would be after your blood.
Peski (*grimacing*) True!
Pariah We have to retrieve that book before they get a chance to use it. We must search the forest until we find them.
Dragonia You and I will attend to that, Pariah.
Peski Jolly good. Have fun. I'll go back to the palace. (*He hastily makes for exit* R)
Dragonia *You will not!* You will remain here. Hide in the cave. If they show up you must get the book from them.
Peski (*wilting*) Oh, I say!
Pariah You can do it, Peski. You're a man!
Dragonia Huh! I would like a second opinion on that! Peski! *Stay!* Come, Pariah!

Dragonia and Pariah exit L

Peski (*miserably*) Being a king isn't as much fun as I thought it would be.

Peski goes into the cave

Little King Cole runs on from up R, *still pursued by the two Creatures. They chase him around, and then out* DL

Florian and Debbie enter from up L, *crossing to exit up* R

Florian (*calling, as they cross*) Your Majesty! ... Where are you? ... Your Majesty!

They exit

Dotty creeps on backwards from L. *She turns slowly, catches sight of the audience and gives a terrified yell*

Dotty Ahhgh!! (*To the audience, relieved*) Oh, it's only you, folks. You did give me a turn. I thought it was the monsters/creatures! Mind you, lookin' at *them* (*pointing to a group*) who can blame me? I haven't been able to find His Little Maj anywhere. Have you seen him?
Audience *Yes!*
Dotty You have! And have the monsters still got him?

Peski emerges from the cave. He creeps up behind Dotty. The audience shouts warnings

What's up?
Audience Behind you! Behind you!
Dotty Behind me? (*Scared*) It's ... It's not a m-m-monster, is it?
Audience *No!*
Dotty What is it then? (*She turns and sees Peski, who is on her left*) Oh! It's only pesky Peski!
Peski Give it to me! *I want it!*
Dotty (*to the audience*) Oh girls! I haven't heard those words for years!
Peski Give me that book!
Dotty (*clutching the book*) No!

Peski grabs the book and tries to pull it away from Dotty

Pariah enters from L. *She grabs Peski around the waist and helps to pull*

Act II, Scene 5

Dragonia enters from L. *She grabs Pariah around the waist and pulls*

Dotty hangs on desperately, but is starting to lose ground

The Fiddlers enter from R. *They form a line behind Dotty and pull*

A frantic tug-o-war ensues. Eventually, Dotty, still in possession of the book, is pulled free. Everyone falls over, Dotty and Fiddlers on R, *Peski, Pariah and Dragonia on* L. *They get to their feet*

While they are getting to their feet, several of the Creatures shamble on at the back

Dotty is the first to see them and lets out a scream

Little King Cole enters from up R. *He is now arm in arm with the two Creatures who had previously been chasing him*

Dotty Your Maj! Stop playin' with those ... those *things!* You don't know where they've been!
Little King Cole It's all right. They're very friendly when you really get to know them. (*To Creatures*) Aren't you?

The Creatures grunt and nod their heads

Yes. We've become great friends. They'd do anything for me.
Dotty In that case, perhaps you'll ask 'em to take charge of those three while we try getting you back to normal.
Little King Cole Good idea! (*To Creatures*) Would you mind? (*Pointing to group* L) Seize them!

Three Creatures grab Peski, Pariah and Dragonia and hold them firmly. Dotty and Little King Cole go up to the cave

Dotty Right, Maj! Let's give it a whirl. In you go!
Little King Cole (*pausing at the entrance*) I'm relying on you to get it right, Dotty.
Pariah (*with a scornful laugh*) Ha! She'll mess it up!
Dotty Don't listen to 'er! I always got top marks for science. In you go!

Little King Cole goes into the cave

(*Calling into the cave*) Are you all right, Yer Maj?

Little King Cole (*from cave. With an echo effect*) Yes ... I'm just getting into the pool ...

A loud splash is heard

(*From the cave*) I'm in! ... Brr! It's cold! ... Over to you, Dotty. Read the spell!
Dotty Right! One spell comin' up! (*With false bravado, she opens the book. After a while she realizes she has it upside down and turns it the right way*)
Pariah Ha! She hasn't got a clue!
Dotty (*frantically turning the pages*) There's got to be something 'ere somewhere!
Little King Cole (*from the cave*) Is there a problem?
Dotty (*calling into the cave, with false bravado*) No. Everything's under control! (*Back to turning pages*) Oh! Where is it? Where is it? ... Ah! What's this? (*Reading*) Spell for reversing age process in magic pool That's it! I've found it!

Florian and Debbie enter from up L

Debbie Mum! What are you doing?
Dotty Debbie! You're just in time to see me perform a miracle.
Florian What's going on here?
Dotty Well, I'm about to ... Oh, just stand back and watch! (*Calling to cave*) Are you ready, Yer Maj?
Little King Cole (*from cave*) Yes! Hurry up! It's freezing in here!
Dotty Right! 'Ere goes! (*Reading from the book*)
        O, Powers of darkness and sorcery!
        Come to my aid and work for me!

There is flash of lightning and a clap of thunder

Looks like we're cookin' with gas! (*She continues to read*)
        He who now bathes in the magic water,
        Wants things back the way they oughter.
Crikey! Who wrote this rubbish! (*She continues to read*)
        So reverse the process quite distinctly,
        And change him back into a wrinkly!

There is a flash from inside the cave

Old King Cole (restored) stumbles out, still wearing his red combinations

Act II, Scene 5   61

Dotty Crikey! It worked!
King Cole By Jove! I'm me again! I'm back to normal. (*He feels and examines his regained physique*)
Dotty Yes. You can honestly say you're *feelin' your* old self again.
King Cole (*shaking her warmly by the hand*) Thank you, Dotty.
Florian Your Majesty. I really have no idea what is going on here, but I always knew you were still with us. (*Pointedly in Peski and Pariah's direction*) Despite what *others* said to the contrary!
King Cole (*moving down to them*) Ah, yes! My dear brother and loving sister-in-law! I'll be having *that* back for a start! (*He whips the crown from Peski's head and places it on his own*) Well! What have you got to say for yourselves?
Peski (*grovelling*) It wasn't me, brother! ... It was all Pariah's idea!
Pariah (*snarling at him*) You ungrateful worm!
King Cole Trying to steal my place on the throne, eh? Isn't that treason, Florian?
Florian It certainly is, Your Majesty.
King Cole And what's the punishment for that?
Florian Beheading, Your Majesty.
Peski (*quacking*) Oooh! You can't do that! I'm your brother!
King Cole True. Then we'll make it life imprisonment. On bread and water!
Pariah You can't do that! I'm wheat intolerant!
Dotty I've got a much better idea, Yer Maj. Why don't you let the punishment fit the crime?
King Cole What had you in mind?

Dotty whispers in the King's ear

An excellent idea! (*To Creatures*) My friends, be so good as to put those two in the cave.

The Creatures drag the protesting pair up to the cave. The King follows them up. Dotty consults the book

Peski (*yelling in terror*) No!... Wait!... What are you going to do?!
King Cole You'll see! Put him in!

The Creature pushes Peski into the cave. A yell, followed by a loud splash is heard

(*To Pariah*) You next!
Pariah (*appealing to Dragonia*) Mamma! Aren't you going to do something to save me?

Dragonia (*unconcerned*) Do I look like Bruce Willis?
King Cole Put her in!

The Creature pushes Pariah into the cave

Pariah exits

A loud splash is heard

Have you found it, Dotty?
Dotty I think so. This ought to do the trick. (*Reading from book*)
O, Powers of darkness and sorcery!
Come to my aid and work for me!

There is a flash of lightning and a clap of thunder. So as not to spoil the surprise, Dotty should only mime reading out the spell. Loud, dramatic music is played over the sound system. Something like Mussorgsky's "Night on Bare Mountain" perhaps? When she has finished "reading", Dotty snaps the book shut. This cues the music to fade out

There is a flash from inside the cave

King Cole (*to Dotty*) Do you think it worked?
Dotty We'll soon find out. Fingers crossed!

Dotty goes into the cave. She re-appears carrying a "baby" in each arm. They are wrapped in shawls of pink and blue. NOTE: If possible it would be nice to hear the "babies" crying!

King Cole Ha! Ha! Success!
Dotty Yes! Here they are! Baby Peski and baby Pariah! We shouldn't have any more trouble from these two. Well, not until they're old enough to go to [local school/college] that is. What d'you want me to do with 'em? They're a bit damp! And I don't think all of it's due to bein' in the pool.
King Cole As he's my brother, I suppose I'm stuck with Peski.

The Herald enters from R

(*To Herald*) Ah! You're just in time. Would you mind taking my baby brother back to the palace?

Dotty tosses "baby" Peski across to the Herald. He just manages to catch it

Act II, Scene 5   63

He sniffs the bundle, makes a wry face, and then exits R, *holding the bundle at arm's length*

The King takes "baby" Pariah from Dotty and moves to Dragonia

King Cole This is yours I believe.
Dragonia *What!* No, thank you!
King Cole You're her mother, aren't you?! Here! (*He thrusts the "baby" into her arms*) And see that you make a better job of bringing her up this time.
Dragonia But ... I don't want to look after a baby at my age!
Dotty (*with relish*) No. Just think of all those sleepless nights! The teething, the nappy changing, the *pong!*
Dragonia (*in utter misery*) Oooo!

Dragonia and bundle exit L

King Cole And now to other matters. Where is Miss Debbie?
Debbie (*coming forward, fearing the worst*) I'm here, Your Majesty.
King Cole Being tricked by those two has made me realize how foolish I have been. It was selfish and ridiculous of me to expect a pretty young girl like you to marry an ugly old crock like me. So, I hereby release you from your obligation.
Debbie (*overjoyed*) Oh, Your Majesty! Do you really mean it?
King Cole Yes. You are now free to fall in love and marry someone of your own choosing.
Florian
Debbie } (*together, rushing into each other's arms*) Darling!
Dotty (*to the audience*) Crikey! That didn't take her long! (*Sidling up to the King*) Er ... Does that mean you're still lookin' for a wife?
King Cole I suppose it does.
Dotty Well, you need look no further. (*She flutters her eyelashes at him*)
King Cole You mean ... you and I ...?
Dotty Yes!
King Cole But ——
Dotty (*nudging him*) Oh, go on! It's still yer birthday! Give yourself a trout ... I mean treat!
King Cole Well, I ... Oh, why not!
Dotty (*punching the air*) *Yes!*
King Cole (*to the audience*) After all, she knows exactly how I like my pancake tossed. (*He goes down on one knee*) Dotty Dumplin, will you do me the great honour of becoming my wife?

Dotty Very nice. Not so much Jane Austen as Austin Powers. It'd be better if you had some clothes on, but ... (*Exuberantly*) *Yes! Yes! A thousand times YES!!*
King Cole Jolly good. (*He has difficulty rising*) Would you mind helping me to get up?
Dotty (*to audience*) Huh! Where've I 'eard *that* before!

Dotty hauls the King to his feet. They embrace. All the others cheer

Song 14

A lively song and dance for all. At the end, the Lights fade to black-out. Music to cover the scene change, and then the Lights come up on —

Scene 6

Outside the Palace Gates

As Act I, Scene 2

Dotty bounces on from DR. *She waves and greets the audience*

Dotty Hello, folks! Hi, kids! Well! What d'you think of that, eh? (*Proudly*) *I'm* going to be a queen! (*To someone*) What was that? You thought I already was! Cheeky monkey! Ooh! I'm so excited! I can't wait for the wedding! I wonder where Kingy's gonna take me for the honeymoon? I hear [local place] is lovely at this time of year ... If you're twenty miles in the opposite direction!

The Fiddlers enter from DL

Look out! Here's the Three Tenors! Or in their case, the Three Fivers!
Fiddlers Congratulations, Dotty.
Dotty Thanks. I bet you're pleased to get your old jobs back.
Fiddlers Yes.
Dotty You'll be able to sing and dance to your hearts' content again.
Fiddlers Yes.
Dotty That'll be nice, won't it?
Fiddlers Yes.
Dotty You don't say much, do you?
Fiddlers No.
Dotty (*archly*) And talkin' of singin', we haven't heard this lot yet, have we?
Fiddlers No.

Act II, Scene 6   65

Dotty (*to the audience*) Ha! Ha! You thought you got away with it, didn't you? Oh, no! Why should we be the only ones to make fools of ourselves. Come on! Let's see what you're made of! (*To someone*) Except *you!* We can all see what *you're* made of! (*To Fiddlers*) Have you got a nice song for them to sing?
Fiddlers Yes.
Dotty And have you got the words?
Fiddlers Yes.
Dotty And will you go and fetch 'em?
Fiddlers Yes.

They exit DL

Dotty (*to the audience*) It's like pullin' teeth!

The Fiddlers return, carrying the song sheets

Oh, yes! A good choice! (*Calling to off stage*) Can you light the candles, please?

The House lights come up

(*To the audience*) Great! Now we can see what you're doin' at the back! Can you all see the words? Right! We'll sing it first, and then you lot can have a go. (*To conductor/pianist*) OK, Sir Elton! Give it some welly!

Song 15

With ad-libs and by-play, they get the audience to sing. If desired, children can be brought up on stage to sing, and then asked their names and ages, etc. (NOTE: Dotty may need to exit for Finale costume change) When the children have returned to their seats, the House lights are taken out

Waving goodbye to the audience, Dotty and the Fiddlers exit DR

At the same time, the Lights fade to black-out

The Herald enters from DL, *illuminated by a spotlight*

He blows an elaborate fanfare. A fanfare sounds. The Herald makes the mistake of lowering his trumpet just before the fanfare has ended!

The Herald gives a "who cares" shrug, and exits DL

The spotlight is taken out, and the Lights come up on —

Scene 7

The Grand Finale

This can be a special Finale setting, or the Palace set can be used. Bright lighting and bouncy music as everyone enters to take their bows. The last to enter are Old King Cole and Dotty. They are both resplendent in regal robes and crowns

Florian	So ends this tale of crowns and kings.
Debbie	Of finding love and the joy it brings.
Dotty	I'm now the wife of Old King Cole.
	I've got me 'ands on his huge bankroll!
King Cole	I'm looking forward to wedded bliss.
	So, come on, Dotty! Give us a kiss!

Dotty kisses his cheek

Dragonia	Ugh! I've never seen such a revolting sight!
Herald	Try lookin' in the mirror late at night!
Peski	With artistic licence we've grown up quick,
Pariah	And we're here to say ...
Peski **Pariah** }	(*together, snarling at the audience*) You make us sick!
Little King Cole	I know in reality I shouldn't be here,
	But as it's panto I'm allowed to appear.
Fiddlers	So, as you homeward ride or stroll,
	It's a fond farewell —
All	(*waving*) From OLD KING COLE!

Song 16

Finale song or a Reprise

Curtain

FURNITURE AND PROPERTY LIST

Further dressing may be added at the director's discretion

ACT I

Scene 1

On stage: Palace interior backcloth
Palace interior wings
Raised area with steps
Dais with throne

Off stage: Trumpet (**Herald**)
Long clay pipe fixed to cushion (**Page**)
Large punch bowl (**Page**)
Prop fiddles (**Fiddlers**)
Trolley. *On it*: large birthday cake with unlit candles and "Happy Birthday" ribbon, knife. (**Dotty**)

Personal: **King Cole**: crown

Scene 2

On stage: Tabs, or front cloth showing palace gates

Off stage: Cake box filled with "Crazy Foam" (**Dotty**)

Scene 3

On stage: Town square backcloth and ground row
House and shop wings
Dress shop wing

Off stage: Trumpet (**Herald**)

Personal: **King Cole**: crown

Scene 4

On stage: Tabs, or Front cloth as Act I, Scene 2

Off stage:	Book of ancient design (**Pariah**)
Personal:	**King Cole**: crown

Scene 5

On stage:	Forbidden Forest backcloth and ground row Forbidden Forest wings Entrance to cave
Off stage:	Book (**Pariah**)
Personal:	**King Cole**: crown

ACT II

Scene 1

On stage:	Town Square as Act I, Scene 3
Off stage:	Trumpet (**Herald**)
Personal:	**Peski**: crown

Scene 2

On stage:	Tabs, or Front cloth as Act 1, Scene 2

Scene 3

On stage:	Palace interior as Act I, Scene 1
Offstage:	Book (**Pariah**) Trolley. *On it*: Huge cake containing child actor playing **Little King Cole** (**Fiddlers**)
Personal:	**Peski**: crown **Pariah**: crown

Scene 4

On stage:	Tabs, or Front cloth as Act 1, Scene 2
Off stage:	Book (**Dragonia**)

Furniture and Property List 69

Scene 5

On stage: Forbidden Forest as Act I, Scene 5

Off stage: Book (**Dotty**)
(In cave) 1 baby doll with blue shawl, 1 baby doll with pink shawl (**Dotty**)

Personal: **Peski**: crown

Scene 6

On stage: Tabs, or front cloth as Act 1, Scene 2

Off stage: Song sheets (**Fiddlers**)

Personal: **Herald**: trumpet

Scene 7 (Finale)

On stage: Special Finale setting or palace interior

LIGHTING PLOT

Property fittings required: shimmering water reflection from inside cave
Various interior and exterior settings.

ACT I, SCENE 1

To open: General interior lighting

| *Cue* 1 | End of Song 3 | (Page 11) |

Fade to black-out

ACT I, SCENE 2

To open: General exterior lighting

| *Cue* 2 | End of Song 4 | (Page 15) |

Fade to black-out

ACT I, SCENE 3

To open: General exterior lighting

Cue 3   Song 6   (Page 17)
Romantic lighting and follow spots

Cue 4   End of Song 6   (Page 17)
Take out romantic lighting and spots. Return to previous setting

Cue 5   Reprise of Song 6 (Optional)   (Page 21)
Romantic lighting and follow spots

Cue 6   End of Reprise (Optional)   (Page 21)
Take out romantic lighting and spots. Return to previous setting

Cue 7   End of Song 7   (Page 23)
Fade to black-out

ACT I, SCENE 4

To open: General exterior lighting

Lighting Plot

Cue 8	**Pariah**: *"The Forbidden Forest!"* *Flash of lightning*	(Page 25)
Cue 9	**Pariah**: *"In — the Forbidden Forest!"* *Flash of lightning*	(Page 26)
Cue 10	**Pariah**: *"To — the Forbidden Forest!"* *Flash of lightning*	(Page 27)
Cue 11	**Pariah** exits *Flash of lightning*	(Page 27)
Cue 12	**Peski** runs out *Fade to black-out*	(Page 27)

ACT I, SCENE 5

To open: Weird and spooky exterior lighting. Water reflection at cave entrance

Cue 13	**Pariah**: *"The Forbidden Forest!"* *Flash of lightning*	(Page 27)
Cue 14	**Pariah**: "Come to my aid and work for me!" *Flash of lightning. Eerie follow spot on* **Pariah**	(Page 30)
Cue 15	Flash from inside cave *Flash of lightning. Take out follow spot*	(Page 30)

ACT II, SCENE 1

To open: General exterior lighting

Cue 16	**Pariah**: *"— the Forbidden Forest!"* *Flash of lightning*	(Page 36)
Cue 17	End of Song 10 *Fade to black-out*	(Page 39)

ACT II, SCENE 2

To open: General exterior lighting

Cue 18	Song 11 *Flashing coloured lights and follow spots for "Rock" number*	(Page 41)
Cue 19	End of Song 11 *Take out flashing lights, spots and return to previous setting*	(Page 41)

Cue 20	**Dotty**, **Little King Cole** and **Fiddlers** exit *Fade to black-out*	(Page 43)

ACT II, SCENE 3

To open: General interior lighting

Cue 21	**Fiddlers** exit *Fade to black-out*	(Page 50)

ACT II, SCENE 4

To open: General exterior lighting, night

Cue 22	**Dragonia**: *"The Forbidden Forest!"* *Flash of lightning*	(Page 51)
Cue 23	**Fiddlers** exit *Fade to black-out*	(Page 53)

ACT II, SCENE 5

To open: Flash of lightning. Weird and spooky lighting, night. Water reflection at cave entrance

Cue 24	Song 13 *Romantic lighting and follow spots*	(Page 55)
Cue 25	End of Song 13 *Take out romantic lighting, spots and return to previous spooky setting*	(Page 55)
Cue 26	**Dotty**: "Come to my aid and work for me!" *Flash of lightning*	(Page 60)
Cue 27	**Dotty**: "Come to my aid and work for me!" *Flash of lightning*	(Page 62)
Cue 28	End of Song 14 *Fade to black-out*	(Page 64)

ACT II, SCENE 6

To open: General exterior lighting

Cue 29	**Dotty**: "Can you light the candles, please?" *Bring up House lights*	(Page 65)

Lighting Plot 73

Cue 30	Children return to their seats *Take out House lights*	(Page 65)
Cue 31	**Dotty** and **Fiddlers** exit *Fade to black-out*	(Page 65)
Cue 32	**Herald** enters *Spotlight on* **Herald**	(Page 65)
Cue 33	**Herald** exits *Take out spotlight*	(Page 66)

ACT II, Scene 4

To open: Bright general lighting. Follow spots

No cues

EFFECTS PLOT

ACT I

Cue 1	**Herald** blows trumpet *Fanfare*	(Page 5)
Cue 2	**Herald** blows trumpet *Fanfare*	(Page 5)
Cue 3	**King Cole**: "She's doing it now" *Flash, followed by loud explosion and billow of smoke (offstage)*	(Page 10)
Cue 4	**Herald** blows trumpet *Fanfare*	(Page 15)
Cue 5	**Pariah**: "*The Forbidden Forest!*" *Clap of thunder*	(Page 25)
Cue 6	**Pariah**: "In — *the Forbidden Forest!*" *Clap of thunder*	(Page 26)
Cue 7	**Pariah**: "To — *the Forbidden Forest!*" *Clap of thunder*	(Page 27)
Cue 8	**Pariah** exits *Clap of thunder*	(Page 27)
Cue 9	To open SCENE 5 *Strange background noises. Ground mist*	(Page 27)
Cue 10	**Pariah**: "*The Forbidden Forest!*" *Clap of thunder*	(Page 27)
Cue 11	**King Cole**: (*from cave*) "No!" *Loud splash from inside cave*	(Page 29)
Cue 12	**Pariah**: "Come to my aid and work for me!" *Clap of thunder*	(Page 30)
Cue 13	**Pariah**: "To turn him into — a *ten-year-old boy!*" *Flash from inside cave. Thunder*	(Page 30)

Effects Plot 75

ACT II

Cue 14	**Herald** blows trumpet *Fanfare*	(Page 34)
Cue 15	**Pariah**: "— *the Forbidden Forest!*" *Clap of thunder*	(Page 36)
Cue 16	Song 11 *Pre-recorded music for "Rock" number.* *Any additional effects required*	(Page 41)
Cue 17	**Dragonia**: "*The Forbidden Forest!*" *Clap of thunder*	(Page 51)
Cue 18	To open SCENE 5 *Clap of thunder. Strange background noises. Ground mist*	(Page 54)
Cue 19	**Little King Cole**: "... I'm just getting into the pool ..." *Loud splash from inside cave*	(Page 60)
Cue 20	**Dotty**: "Come to my aid and work for me!" *Clap of thunder*	(Page 60)
Cue 21	**Dotty**: "And change him back into a wrinkly!" *Flash from inside cave*	(Page 60)
Cue 22	**Creature** pushes **Peski** into cave. **Peski** yells *Loud splash from inside cave*	(Page 61)
Cue 23	**Creature** pushes **Pariah** into cave *Loud splash from inside cave*	(Page 62)
Cue 24	**Dotty**: "Come to my aid and work for me!" *Clap of thunder. Pre-recorded loud dramatic music*	(Page 62)
Cue 25	**Dotty** snaps book shut *Fade out dramatic music. Flash from inside cave*	(Page 62)
Cue 26	**Dotty** brings "babies" from cave *Babies crying*	(Page 62)
Cue 27	**Herald** blows trumpet *Elaborate fanfare*	(Page 65)

www.ingramcontent.com/pod-product-compliance
Ingram Content Group UK Ltd.
Pitfield, Milton Keynes, MK11 3LW, UK
UKHW021844210426
5322IPUK00022B/467